THE
GOD
JOURNEY

Discovering What It's All About

Kyle,
Wishing you abundant
joy and success in your
journey, Ricky
Tutor

Ricky Tutor

Trilogy Christian Publishers
A Wholly Owned Subsidiary of Trinity Broadcasting Network
2442 Michelle Drive
Tustin, CA 92780

Scripture quotations marked NASB are taken from the New American Standard Bible®, copyright © 1960 by The Lockman Foundation. Used by permission.

For information, address Trilogy Christian Publishing
Rights Department, 2442 Michelle Drive, Tustin, Ca 92780.
Trilogy Christian Publishing/ TBN and colophon are trademarks of Trinity Broadcasting Network.

For information about special discounts for bulk purchases, please contact Trilogy Christian Publishing.

Manufactured in the United States of America

Trilogy Disclaimer: The views and content expressed in this book are those of the author and may not necessarily reflect the views and doctrine of Trilogy Christian Publishing or the Trinity Broadcasting Network.

10 9 8 7 6 5 4 3 2 1

Library of Congress Cataloging-in-Publication Data is available.

ISBN 978-1-64773-604-0 (Print Book)
ISBN 978-1-64773-605-7 (ebook)

Contents

Introduction

MY PARENTS BECAME Christians when I was a child. I was brought up in church and was taught that there is a heaven and a hell. But I didn't take God very seriously when I was a child. I slept during the church services whenever I could, and by the time I was a teenager, I remember how I would bring my bag of marijuana and would show it off to my friends in Sunday school.

I was a troublemaker in my early teenage years. My lifestyle revolved around fighting, stealing, drugs, and alcohol. I lived by my feelings. If it felt good, whether it was right or wrong, I wanted to do it. I stood against those who were in authority, and I engaged in destructive actions without giving much thought to the outcome.

But then there came a time when the subject of hell began weighing very heavily on my mind. I remember thinking, *If I get into a fight with somebody and they pull out a knife and stab me and I die, I'm going to hell.* I realized I was playing Russian roulette with my eternity.

Finally, the day came when I chose to repent. The word *repent* means "a change of mind or conversion." It is changing your attitude and ways by making a complete turnaround from your old way of living to God's way.

In September of 1980, at sixteen years old, I decided to take the God journey. I crossed over into the safety zone where my sins were forgiven. What a wonderful feeling it is to be in the peace, safety, and security of being on God's side of the line.

Then my desire to find out what it's all about began to grow. I was now ready to embark upon a journey of discovery that continues to this very day. I got the coffee ready. I grabbed my Bible, pencil, and paper, and I sat at the kitchen table. With soft music playing in the background, I began the journey. My dad was getting ready to go to bed for the night, and when he got up the next morning and was getting ready for work, he was surprised to find me still in my studies.

Eventually, I did something that was a little radical. Because my bedroom was small, I had my bed removed and replaced it with a couch. I slept, prayed, and studied on that couch. My parents became concerned about me because I would often shut myself in my room for hours. I realized that God's way is the right way from the very beginning. I invested many hours in my effort to learn more about God and His way of doing things.

My Calling

When I was seventeen years old, the Lord began revealing to me that there was something He wanted me to do. During an evening church service, a woman came over to where I was seated and asked if she could pray for me. I let her know that would be fine. After she prayed, she said, "God told me to tell you not to be impatient. He is going to use you."

This was coming from a quiet, gentle woman who loved God and was known for her spirituality. But how could I know she really heard from God? The Bible tells us, "In the mouth of two or three witnesses, let every word be established." God confirms every fact by the testimony of two or three witnesses. In other words, if your first witness was truly of God, He will confirm it with other witnesses down the road.

The Second Witness

I believe it was around a year later when I was attending a different church that a woman, I did not know approached me and asked if she could pray for me. I let her know that would be fine. After she prayed, she said, "God told me to tell you that He did not lie. He is going to use you."

I don't know if this lady had ever been used by God to do anything like this before. She was so overwhelmed that she stood in front of the church and pointed to where I was seated and said, "I don't know that young boy over there, but God is going to use that boy."

I began sharing these experiences with my mother, and it sparked something in her memory. When she was just a young girl, she doesn't know why she prayed this: she prayed that, one day, God would give her a son who would do a work for God. Were these experiences I was going through the result of a young girl's prayer? I don't know. But it sure seems to fit the puzzle.

The Third Witness

I went for many years not knowing what God wanted me to do. All I knew is that I had a constant desire to continue making further advancement in discovering what it's all about.

Years later, I was attending a different church from the previous two, and once again, God reminded me that He had a purpose for my life. At church this evening, Pastor Tim Bagwell from Lone Tree, Colorado, was our guest speaker.

After Pastor Bagwell completed his sermon, he called me out in front of the hundreds who were in attendance. "Middle section, fourth row. You're in a black-and-white golf shirt, and you have a beard. Come up here. You want this."

This man doesn't know me. What does he want to talk to me about?

So, I walked to the front and stood before him, and he said, "Let me explain something. God is getting ready to absolutely do something in you because you have a date with destiny. There is a purpose of God on your life. God appointed you to have an anointing over your life."

Pastor Bagwell said many things that I will reveal later in the book, but another thing I will share with you right now is that he said, "God has placed a proclaiming anointing upon your life."

The word anointing refers to a God-given ability. Without doing a study of the word proclaim, I automatically thought it meant preaching. The idea of delivering sermons in front of an assembly of people bothered me. I am normally a quiet type of person who keeps to himself. I am a thinker—one who thinks deeply and seriously. I would rather think than talk.

When my wife and I began going together, she began seeing the type of person that I am, and she would refer to me as a hermit. A hermit is one who likes to be alone, far from people, sometimes because of their religious beliefs or maybe because they simply want some privacy. So again, this whole idea of preaching in church bothered me.

About five years later, I wrote my first book entitled *What It's All About*. It later expanded into a larger book called *Doing the Will of the Father*. As I was writing this book, the thought came to me to study the definition of the word *proclaim*. I looked in Webster's Dictionary and found that the word proclaim means "to declare publicly in either speech or by writing."

I looked up the word in my thesaurus, and it said that it means "to publish." Then I looked up the word *publish*, and it read "to proclaim." After I found this out, I laughed, realizing that I was doing exactly what I am supposed to be doing. My calling is to follow my passion in discovering what the God journey is all about and then simply share it with others by publishing my writing.

SECTION ONE

Crossing Over

Chapter One

I Was A Troublemaker

DURING MY FIRST year in junior high, while in sixth grade, I joined the sport of wrestling. I joined the sport to be the wrestling manager, I suppose, because I wasn't confident enough to be a wrestler.

But then something happened that changed the way I saw myself. In fact, it changed the course of my life. During gym class, the teacher announced that the activity of the day would be the sport of wrestling. The star athlete was a boy named Billy.

At my school, students were not allowed to join the sport of wrestling until they were in sixth grade. But Billy came from a different organization where you were allowed to join at a much younger age. He had years of wrestling experience. So, the eyes of the class were focused on him because if you want to learn how to wrestle, "Watch Billy!"

The students gathered around the wrestling mat with Billy at the center, and guess who they chose to wrestle Billy—the shy, timid, lacking-in-confidence wrestling manager. So, I started wrestling Billy, and to my amazement, I was beating him. Billy then whispered in my ear, "Let me win."

Suddenly, a light came on. I had an ability that I didn't know I had. Self-confidence arose inside me, and from that day forth, being a wrestling manager was a thing of the past. I became a wrestler, and by the time I was in eighth grade, I did something that nobody had previously done in that school. I went the entire year undefeated, and for my last wrestling match, I was going for first place in the state of Illinois.

My last wrestling opponent, whom I later found out had flunked a year and was already supposed to be in high school, managed to outpoint me in my final wrestling match of the year. But what I achieved in wrestling those three short years, going from a wrestling manager to a second-in-state winner, gave me a firm belief in my own ability and helped to prepare me for my next big challenge.

Fighting the Bully

One day, I walked into the school restroom and saw something that was very appalling to me. I watched a bully named Keith grab the head of another student and violently bang it against the sink.

My earliest memories of Keith went back to grade school. We went to a school where physical pain was used as a method to punish and correct the students. I witnessed one teacher slap a student on the back and whack a student's hands with a ruler. Another teacher would slap you in the face, and another teacher would make an example out of you by bringing you in front of the class and giving you the paddle.

The threat of physical pain was enough to persuade most of our class to stay within the boundaries and avoid these kinds of teacher confrontations. But Keith was a different story. He would defy the odds. Our class would watch in amazement as this headstrong and determined-to-have-his-own-way little boy would stand up to our teacher with angry defiance.

While Keith did what he could to have his own way in class, he dominated the playground. He seemed to get a lot of pleasure out of punching the other students to show them who is boss. But I had an advantage over him. I could outrun him. I found out that the only way I could keep from being hit by Keith was to outrun him.

Then in our junior high years, Keith became bigger, stronger, and brashly self-confident. If there was something he didn't like about you, he would let you know about it. It seems that he would choose from four different categories—tell you what he thinks about you, punch you, beat you, or challenge you to an after-school fight.

Finally, the day came when I became his target. He was seated at the desk next to me when he assaulted me with the obscenest words I had ever heard before. Using the F-word, he asked me if I had sex with my own mother. I then proceeded to kick his desk and said to him, "After school!"

The news spread around about the big fight. When school was over, we walked outside, and a crowd of students followed us as we began our search for a secluded place to fight.

I could feel the adrenaline pumping. I was no longer the same person who ran from him in grade school. I was no longer the wrestling manager who was unsure of himself. Several years of physical exercise, training, and achievement had now placed me in a position of strength. It was time for me to redeem myself.

When we found a secluded area, the crowd gathered around, with me and Keith in the center. Then two words came out of Keith's mouth: "No wrestling!" I knew I had the advantage. This was the day when I discovered by experience that a wrestler who can fight has the upper hand over a person who is merely tough with his fists. Simply take them down to the ground, and you have them where you want them.

Friends with the Bully

Not too long after our fight, Keith and I became friends. We respected each other's strength. I admired him for his courage to take a stand against those who are in authority and his guts to engage in destructive actions without giving much thought to the outcome. He was better than me in that regard.

By hanging around Keith, I was introduced to things I had never experienced before. One day, I followed him to the back of our school where we would look through a broken glass window and watch the girls in their locker room. Another day, I followed him into a Laundromat where he snatched a roll of coins from a woman when she wasn't looking.

Then we entered high school and began doing drugs together. We would go across the street during lunch break, get high, and then return to school to finish the school day.

I remember one particular day when we were sitting on top of a store across the street from our school, buzzing on LSD (which probably explains why we were sitting on top of the store) when from a distance, we could see one of the biggest guys in our school walking toward the store.

When he saw us sitting on top of the store, he began picking up rocks and hurling them at us and mouthing off at us continually until he finally entered the store. Keith then said to me, "Ricky, are you going to let him get away with that?"

I wasn't crazy about facing this big guy, but I didn't want to look like a wimp in front of Keith either, so I jumped down and waited for him to come out. When he finally came out, he looked down at me and proceeded to degrade me with obscene words. Then without saying a word, I attacked him with everything I had within me, and to my amazement, the fight was over within a matter of seconds. I found out later that he had to get stitches in his mouth.

This experience only added to my self-confidence. But my self-confidence started turning into prideful cockiness. I became overly convinced of my own superiority. I wreaked havoc on my teachers with my don't-tell-me-what-to-do attitude, which resulted in suspensions time and again.

A Thief in the Making

I began taking things that didn't belong to me—things like my dad's car. Being bored with school, I went up to my friend John with what I thought was a good idea. "John, let's run away. I'll take my dad's car and pick you up, and we'll take off to another state."

So, I got up in the middle of the night, pushed my dad's car to the road so he wouldn't hear the car when it started, and then took off to John's house and waited for him. I waited and waited for him until I finally decided to go back home. John either had no intention of running away, or maybe he heard the principal's warning: "Stay away from Ricky Tutor because he is heading for prison!"

I began stealing from relatives and stores and then added the next-door neighbor to my list. We lived out in the country, surrounded by fields with only one neighbor who lived behind us. So, I decided to start stealing from that neighbor. Sometimes I would go in and take things such as pornographic magazines. Another day, I took a fifth of whiskey from his home and went a couple of miles down the road, away from the view of my parents, to a secluded place next to a field where I drank about half the bottle in a matter of minutes. At fourteen years old, I didn't know I was overdoing it until it was too late. I alternated back and forth from lying in the field to walking until I finally made it home and went to bed.

School Dropout

Then came my last day of high school. I had a disagreement with my shop class teacher where I proceeded to shove him, and he pushed me back. The shoving match led to the principal showing up to tell me I was suspended. I then walked across the street to the pay phone, called my mother, and told her, "I'm not going back to school. If you try to make me, I'm running away." Then my mom, being the easygoing person she is (unless you get her angry), agreed that I wouldn't have to go back.

It was against the law for me to quit school at the age of fifteen, but the principal told my dad he wouldn't report it until I turned sixteen. It seemed the principal was willing to break the law to keep me out of their school.

Then it was time for me to look for a job. My first job was at a motel restaurant, where I worked as a busboy. As a busboy, I would clean off the tables and steal tips at the same time. I was eventually fired for putting hot sauce in a fellow employee's soft drink and smoking marijuana on the job.

My next job was at a pizza restaurant, where I worked as a dishwasher. I was eventually fired for drinking their beer and getting into a fight with a customer—literally fighting the customer on the floor of the restaurant.

I lived by my feelings. If it felt good, whether it was right or wrong, I wanted to do it. I stood against those who were in authority, and I engaged in destructive actions without giving much thought to the outcome. I damaged mailboxes because I wanted to. While sitting on a train, I turned around and punched a hole in the wall because I felt like it.

One evening, I was out past the curfew. I walked into Coney Island restaurant and walked over to a man sitting on a stool and said to him, "Hey, man, you have a joint I can buy off you?" He then proceeded to give me a smart-aleck answer and gesture. I then gave him one more chance to answer me correctly, and when he failed, I knocked him to the ground and fought him on the floor of the restaurant. They then locked the door of the restaurant and kept me in until the police arrived, put me in handcuffs, and hauled me to the police station.

Fighting, stealing, drugs and alcohol—this was my way of life. Then my lifestyle as a thief began escalating from stealing from my relatives, neighbors, and stores to coming up with what I thought was a good idea. My plan was to go out at night, beat people over the head, and take their wallets. It seemed like an easy way to make money.

I remember thinking, *If I hit them hard enough to kill them, nobody will know it anyway because it will be dark out. I* had my club ready and was all set to go.

Chapter Two

My Conversion

IT SEEMS THAT the principal was foretelling my future when he said that I was heading for prison. But then one day, my dad told me there was something he wanted me to watch on TV. He made me listen to a preacher by the name of Billy Graham. At first, I didn't like the idea; but then I started listening, and his words concerning God and the Bible began sounding so clear to me.

My parents became Christians when I was a child. I was brought up in church and was taught that God is real and that there is a heaven and a hell. But I didn't take God very seriously when I was a child. I slept during the church services whenever I could, and by the time I reached my teenage years, I remember how I would bring my bag of marijuana to church and would show it off to my friends in Sunday school.

But now at this juncture of my life, I was aroused by a spark of curiosity. In fact, I took my parents' large family Bible without them knowing it and placed it under my bed so when I had time alone, I could investigate this book. I took their Bible without them knowing it because I didn't want them to think I had any desire for this Bible stuff.

Then I was disappointed when Mom found the Bible. Mom was accustomed to finding certain items hidden in my room—things like marijuana, pot pipes, and pornographic magazines. So, you could imagine how surprised she was to find the Bible hidden in my room.

Looking back, it seems that the question in my heart was "What is it all about?" I needed to know what the game plan for life was. The way I played the game of life was to live by my feelings. I lived by the motto that says, "If it feels good, do it."

When I found time alone, I started reading at the beginning of the Bible where it said, "In the beginning God created the heaven and the earth" (Genesis 1:1).

It went on to talk about what God did day after day to make a perfect world for His children. It was fascinating for me to find out how it all began. If this was telling me how it all began, it would surely tell me what it's all about, what our purpose is for being here, and where we're going.

I recall one night after my parents went to bed; I went to the living room and turned on the TV to the Christian station. These were the days when most homes had only one TV. I listened to a preacher by the name of Rex Humbard. As I was listening, I remember how a force of love came through the TV and seemed to penetrate my heart. I could feel it on my flesh.

During this time, I kept one ear on my parents' bedroom. When it sounded like they were getting up, I would quickly change the channel. I didn't want them to think I had any desire for this Christian stuff.

I became interested in God and the Bible and was curious to find out what it's all about. It was on my mind so much that when I was out partying with my friends, I would bring up the subject of God into our conversation.

At times, I would lie on the floor, high on drugs or drunk on alcohol (or both at the same time), and I remember the light that began to shine in my darkness. I would think about the Christians. There seemed to be a glow about them. There was something that caused them to be joyful and happy. When I compared their lives to mine, I felt so dirty and so unclean on the inside.

In the meantime, I continued in my troublemaking ways. One day, I was walking through the mall with my friend Keith when I spontaneously began pushing him into people. Then he, in turn, would push me into others who were passing by. We alternated back and forth, trying to start a fight, until somebody took me up on it. We walked outside to begin our fight when I noticed him reaching into his pocket to grab what I believed was a knife, so I kicked him in the area where they say, "it counts," and he changed his mind about pulling it out.

The Subject of Hell

It was around this time when the subject of hell began bothering me. I remember thinking, *If I get into a fight with somebody and they pull out a knife and stab me and I die, I'm going to hell.* I realized I was playing Russian roulette with my eternity.

I was now becoming desperate to cross over onto God's side of the line. I was interested in God. I was curious to find out what it's all about, and I was afraid of spending eternity in hell. But there was something holding me back. What will people think about me? My life was about being tough and strong, and I was concerned about looking soft and weak.

Then one day, I watched a movie that gave me an idea. The movie was called *The Ten Commandments*. In the movie, Moses went up into a mountain where he experienced the tangible presence of Almighty God. Then after spending time in God's presence, he began descending the mountain, and his face was literally glowing as a result of being exposed to the glory of God.

This experience made a strong impression on me. I found it to be extremely awesome. It also gave me an idea. This was how I could get acquainted with God without anybody knowing. I started tying weights around my body and walked up and down the road, preparing myself to take a Bible and everything I needed up into a mountain to stay there for a while in order to get acquainted with God.

But thank God, God saw my heart and sent somebody my way. My uncle came over with a young teenager whose name was Steve. He was one of the tenants who stayed in my uncle's home. Steve, whom I later found out was a Christian, said he could get me a job working where he worked as a dishwasher at the Holiday Inn.

So, I started working with him, and I remember saying the F-word in front of him, and he let me know right away, "Man, you need Jesus!" I then began sharing with him my desire to cross over to God's side.

It was at this time that I saw an opening. I found a way that helped me to finally make the decision. I also moved in with my uncle and got away from my familiar surroundings and chose to be a Christian. I received Jesus as my Lord and Savior in September 1980 at sixteen years old.

Water Baptism

I then qualified for water baptism. The Bible is clear that Christians should be baptized. It's not something we do in order to be saved, but it's something we do because we are saved and because Jesus commanded it.

When an individual receives Jesus, he or she becomes inwardly cleansed from sin. Then water baptism is to follow afterward because water baptism is an outward symbol of an inward cleansing.

Chapter Three

The Journey Begins

I CROSSED OVER INTO the safety zone where my sins were forgiven. I was given a second chance—a new beginning! What a wonderful feeling it is to be in the peace, safety, and security of being on God's side of the line.

When my dad found out about my decision for Christ, he came over to my uncle's home and presented me with a gift. It was my very first Bible. I still have this Bible in my possession, and while the pages have now turned yellow, it stands as a memorial of when I began my journey with God.

One of the things I love about crossing over onto God's side of the line is that I now have directions for life. I found out that God did not create this whole world without giving us some instructions. He gave us the Bible to be our map and guide for this life's journey. It tells us how to keep our thoughts, words, and actions within the right boundaries, and it tells us how to receive God's forgiveness when we should cross over those boundaries. In short, the Bible reveals the boundaries for living, and there is safety in those boundaries.

It wasn't too long after this that I decided to move back in with my parents. Then my desire to find out what it's all about began to grow. I was now ready to embark upon a journey of discovery that continues to this very day.

I got the coffee ready. I grabbed my Bible, pencil, paper, and I sat at the kitchen table. With soft music playing in the background, I began the journey. My dad was getting ready to go to bed for the night, and when he got up the next morning and was getting ready for work, he was surprised to find me still in my studies.

Eventually, I did something that was a little radical. Because my bedroom was small, I had my bed removed and replaced it with a couch. I slept, prayed, and studied on that couch. My parents became concerned about me because I would often shut myself in my room for hours.

I realized that God's way is the right way from the very beginning. I invested many hours in my effort to learn more about God and His way of doing things.

The Presence of God

For you to understand what I am about to share with you next, I need to spend some time talking to you about the presence of God. First, let's talk about God's omnipresence. The word omnipresence means "being in all places at all times." I realized early on that God is not just way up there in heaven; He fills every space and is as close to me as the breath that I breathe. David, the psalmist said,

> Where can I go from your spirit? Or where can I flee from your presence? If I go up to heaven, you are there, if I go down to the place of the dead, you are there. I could ask the darkness to hide me and the light around me to become night but even in darkness I cannot hide from you. To you the

night shines as bright as day. Darkness
and light are both alike to you.

Psalm 139:7–8, 11–12

Second, there is His manifest presence. The word
manifest means "to bring from the unseen, unheard, or
unknown into the seen, heard, or known." This is when
our mind and senses become aware of His nearness. In the
Bible, we find that some saw Him, that others heard His
voice without seeing Him, while others sensed His nearness and immediately knew things they never knew before.

All through the Bible, from beginning to end, God
reveals His passionate desire for man and His pursuit of
man. It is a fact that God wants to draw near to us even
more than we want to draw near to Him.

The Bible tells us that God yearns for us (James
4:5). The word yearn means "to long for intensely." This
has been God's deepest cry of the heart since the beginning of time. God's heart cry throughout the ages are for
people who would desire to know Him in response to
His desire for us!

God Inhabits Our Praise

I found out early on that when you don't know what to pray about, you can spend much time in thanksgiving and praise unto God. I would also spend much of my prayer time singing unto the Lord. I know this may sound kind of strange, but I learned this in church. During the praise and worship part of a church service, we sing songs. Some songs we sing directly to God, while others are about God and what He has promised us in His Word.

The Bible tells us to

> Serve the Lord with gladness; come before Him with joyful singing. Know that the Lord Himself is God; It is He who has made us, and not we ourselves; we are His people and the sheep of His pasture. Enter His gates with thanksgiving and His courts with praise. Give thanks to Him, bless His name.
>
> Psalm 100:2–4

I remember one day as I drew near to God in praise, a force of love began welling up inside me. It was a strong feeling of unconditional love. It felt like I could take every person of this world into my arms, regardless of who they are and what they have done, and embrace them.

When my prayer time was completed, I got up and noticed that the intensity of that love went away. I was confused by this experience. I reasoned that perhaps God was showing me the level of love I could grow and develop into.

Eventually, I realized that there was a connection between praising God and the presence of God. So, I began playing praise and worship music on my stereo and would get on my knees and sing along with those songs in praise unto God. Then I noticed that the atmosphere in my room seemed to be charged with love and tranquility. This presence caused me to be full of joy.

As I continued in my studies, I found the promise in scripture that says, "Draw near to God and He will draw near to you" (James 4:8). Another verse tells us that "God inhabits the praises of His people" (Psalm 22:3).

When you do a study of the original Hebrew language from where this verse came from, it tells us that God takes a seat in the midst of His people who praise Him, and still another portion of scripture tells us that "in His presence is fullness of joy" (Psalm 16:11). When it comes to the subject of love, not only does God have love but the Bible also tells us, "God is love" (1 John 4:8).

When I brought these four verses together, they fit like a puzzle. They revealed to me that God, who is love, would take a seat as I took the time to praise Him. As I drew near to Him, He would draw near to me, and the love that I was feeling was the love that He has for every person upon the face of this earth. I would then be enraptured in His presence, and His presence caused me to be full of joy.

Chapter Four

The Holy Spirit

ONE OF THE things I found out after crossing over onto God's side of the line is that I was no longer alone. When an individual chooses to put his or her trust in Jesus, he or she becomes what the Bible calls *born again.* Being born again is not just an experience. Rather, it is receiving the indwelling presence of the Holy Spirit, a divine personality who comes to make His home in us.

There are three different ways that God reveals Himself. He reveals Himself as God, the Father, His Son, Jesus, and the Holy Spirit. These are three different expressions of God, just as thoughts, spoken words, and written words are three different expressions of every person.

Every one of us is a spirit being living inside this body of flesh, bone, and muscle. When God speaks to an individual, He speaks to him or her by His Holy Spirit. He speaks to them Spirit to spirit. God is a communicator who desires interaction. One of the major characteristics that differentiates God, our Father, from false gods and idols are that God, the Creator of all things, speaks!

Only on rare occasions will God speak to His people in an audible voice. The primary way God speaks to His people is by an inward witness. He bears witness with our spirit. As for me, most of the time, it is sort of like a "hunch," or one of those something-tells-me type of situations. At other times, He may speak with a few words or sentences. But He will never say anything to you that doesn't line up with the written Word, so studying the Bible is essential to you recognizing His voice.

Let me give you an example. I began praying every day: "Lord, make me a winner of thousands of souls." I would pray this day after day until one day, my prayer was interrupted with these penetrating thoughts: "This is how you can become a winner of thousands of souls—through prayer. It's not only because of preachers preaching the gospel that people are being saved. But it's because of the prayers of the saints."

I was like—what was that! Then I began realizing that it was the Holy Spirit. Then I found a place in the Bible where Jesus said, "The harvest is plentiful, but the laborers are few; therefore pray earnestly to the Lord of the harvest to send out laborers into his harvest" (Matt. 9:37–38).

Jesus was talking about Christian laborers and the harvest of lost souls. God is the proprietor of the great harvest of the world, and He can only send people to gather it in. We are to pray that many would be raised up and sent forth, who will labor in bringing souls to Christ.

The Farmer's Vision

I am reminded of a farmer who had a great desire to be a missionary, but God never called him to this work. So, he did the next best thing: he dedicated his life to praying and interceding in prayer for missionaries.

One day, while this farmer was in prayer, God showed him a vision. In this vision, he saw a woman missionary and a man who was close by and was about to make his attempt to kill her. Suddenly, while the farmer was seeing this vision, the farmer was transported from where he was into the vision where the missionary was. He then stepped between the missionary and the man attempting to kill her, and the man fled.

About two years later, the farmer came in late for church one day, and to his surprise, he saw that same woman missionary giving her testimony to the church about what she experienced two years ago, when a man attempted to kill her. But then somebody stepped between them and saved her life.

When she finished telling her story, the farmer stood up trembling and said to the woman, "Lady, do you know me?"

She said, "You're the one!"

The Holy Spirit and Persecuted Believers

Years ago, when Russian believers didn't have the freedom to worship like they do today, they had to go to hidden places to gather to have their church services. From time to time, they would have to change the location of their meeting places because they would get raided by the KGB.

Then there came a time when the KGB continually found their hiding places, and they realized that there was a spy among them. There was someone among them who pretended to be a Christian who continually informed the KGB where their meetings would be.

Knowing that the Holy Spirit is only inside real Christians, they made an announcement. Everybody was going to have to find out from the Holy Spirit where the next meeting was going to be. So, the next time they gathered, everybody showed up except for one. Then they knew who the impostor was.

The Holy Spirit in the Life of Jesus

A miracle took place two thousand years ago. God Almighty laid aside His glory and appeared on earth as a man.

For a brief time in His earthly existence, He humbled Himself of His divinity and literally became a man in every way. This was precisely what happened the day Jesus was born in Bethlehem. He humbled Himself to the level and status of man to become equal with the ones He created.

In coming from heaven to this earth, He laid aside His godlike qualities. He emptied Himself and laid aside omnipresence—which means "everywhere present" to inhabit a body, He received from His Heavenly Father and the Virgin Mary.

He emptied Himself and laid aside omnipotence, which means "all powerful." Jesus said,

> Truly, truly, the Son can do nothing
> of Himself, unless it is something, He
> sees the Father doing; for whatever the
> Father does, these things the Son also
> does in like manner. I can do nothing
> on my own initiative.
>
> John 5:19, 30

Jesus confessed and made it clear that while He lived on earth, He was an agent of the Father and did not work independently from Him. All the works Jesus did was through the anointing of the Holy Spirit that His Father placed on Him. Scripture declares,

> You know of Jesus of Nazareth, how
> God anointed Him with the Holy
> Spirit and with power, and how He

went about doing good and healing all who were oppressed by the devil, for God was with Him.

Acts 10:38

He emptied Himself and laid aside omniscience, which means "all knowing." Jesus said,

> For the Father loves the Son and shows Him all things that He Himself is doing; and the Father will show Him greater works than these, so that you will marvel. For I did not speak on my own initiative, but the Father Himself who sent me has given me a commandment as to what to say and what to speak.
>
> John 5:20, 12:49

Jesus declared that the Father would show Him greater things—in other words, things He did not see or know when He spoke these words.

During His entire earthly journey, He did not lean on any of His own godlike qualities. He came to show us by example how to be obedient to the Heavenly Father, in total reliance on the Holy Spirit, to overcome and be victorious in every area of life.

Throughout the earthly ministry of Jesus, the Holy Spirit was His partner. Jesus and the Holy Spirit always worked together. Jesus was conceived of the Holy Spirit, empowered by the Holy Spirit, led by the Holy Spirit. He healed people by the power of the Holy Spirit, cast out demons by the power of the Holy Spirit, and He was resurrected and seated at God's own right hand through the power of the Holy Spirit.

The Holy Spirit, Our Partner

Now let me explain to you why God places His Holy Spirit inside the spirit of every born-again Christian. For three years, before Jesus went to the cross, He had a close relationship with His disciples. For three years, Jesus was right by their side.

Just as Jesus totally relied on and was dependent on the Holy Spirit, the disciples totally relied on and were dependent on Jesus. Jesus was their comforter, partner, spiritual father, and teacher.

As a result of the disciples having this close relationship with Jesus, their lives were filled with adventure, excitement, joy, victory, power, healings, and miracles. For three years, the disciples relied on and had grown dependent on the physical, visible presence of Jesus.

Then Jesus began revealing to His disciples that He was going to be leaving them soon. He was going to die on the cross for the sins of the whole world and then go back to heaven where He came from.

If you were one of His disciples at that time, you would probably think, *how could you leave us at a time like this? We need you. Please don't abandon us. Don't forsake us.*

Jesus says to His disciples, "I will not leave you comfortless: I will come to you" (John 14:18).

The word comfortless comes from the Greek word *orphanos*, which is where we get the word orphans. This word was used in the New Testament times to describe children who were abandoned by their parents and was also used to describe students who were forsaken by their teachers. Just as children are dependent on their parents, students are dependent on their teachers to teach, guide, and prepare them for life.

Jesus was a spiritual father to His disciples. He knew they were completely reliant on Him. They couldn't make it on their own in the world without Him. That's why Jesus promised them, "I will not leave you like orphans."

So, if Jesus was not going to leave His disciples behind like orphans, what was He going to do for them? Jesus said, "I will pray to the Father, and He is going to give you another Comforter, that He may abide with you forever" (John 14:16).

The word another comes from the Greek word *allos*, which means "one of the very same kind, same character, same everything, or nearly a duplicate."

We find in the very next verse that the Comforter that Jesus was talking about was the Holy Spirit. Jesus was saying that the Holy Spirit that would be sent to them would be like Jesus in every way. The Holy Spirit would be identical to Jesus in the way He speaks and the way He acts. Jesus wanted the disciples to know that following the Holy Spirit wouldn't be any different than following Him. The only difference is that following the Holy Spirit's leadership would be invisible, while the leadership of Jesus was visible.

Scripture declares, "The grace of the Lord Jesus Christ, and the love of God, and the communion of the Holy Ghost, be with you all" (2 Corinthians 13:14).

The word communion comes from the Greek word *koinonia*. This Greek word has a whole flavor of meanings, but one primary meaning is that of partnership. The Holy Spirit is given to every believer, every follower of Jesus Christ to be their partner in this life's journey.

Jesus needed the partnership of the Holy Spirit in order to accomplish His divine role on earth. Since Jesus needed this ongoing partnership with the Holy Spirit, believers—followers of Jesus Christ—absolutely need this ongoing partnership as well.

Jesus referred to the Holy Spirit as Comforter. The word comforter comes from the Greek word *parakaleo*. A study of the word parakaleo teaches us that the Holy Spirit has a calling. Just as many people receive a calling from God to do a specific work, a calling has been placed on the Holy Spirit.

The Holy Spirit has been called to be right beside the believers—to not only be beside them, but to be inside them (John 14:17). He is called to be as close to them as He can possibly get. He is called to become one with them.

The word parakaleo can also be translated as "helper," "standby," "best friend," "personal advisor," "instructor," or "coach." He is a person with all the emotions, personality, and attributes of such a person. He is an intelligent living entity with free will, someone possessing personal properties, having character, and able to think and speak.

Since the Holy Spirit is a person, you can develop a partnership with Him. The key to living a successful Christian life is in yielding our lives to the Holy Spirit and allowing Him to do the work through us. The Holy Spirit's calling is to help us get the job done.

Chapter Five

My Calling

WHEN I WAS seventeen years old, the Lord began revealing to me that He had placed a calling on my life. During an evening church service, a woman came over to where I was seated and asked if she could pray for me. I let her know that would be fine. After she prayed, she said, "God told me to tell you not to be impatient. He is going to use you."

This was coming from a quiet, gentle woman who loved God and was known for her spirituality. But how could I know if she really heard from God? The Bible tells us, "In the mouth of two or three witnesses let every word be established" (2 Corinthians 13:1). God confirms every fact by the testimony of two or three witnesses. In other words, if your first witness was truly of God, He will confirm it with other witnesses down the road.

The Second Witness

I believe it was around a year later when I was attending a different church that a woman, whom I did not know, approached me and asked if she could pray for me. I let her know that would be fine. After she prayed, she said, "God told me to tell you that He did not lie. He is going to use you."

I don't know if this lady had ever been used by God to do anything like this before. She was so overwhelmed that she stood in front of the congregation who were assembled, pointed over to where I was seated, and said, "I don't know that young boy over there, but God is going to use that boy!"

The Leaping Verse

Then one day, I was reading in the Bible in 1 Corinthians 15, and when I got to the fifty-eighth verse, this verse leaped out at me. I don't mean this as a figure of speech. I mean, this verse leaped out at me!

The best way to describe it is, it was sort of like being at the movies, where you wear 3-D glasses and various scenes of the movie leap out at your face. This is what I mean when I say the fifty-eighth verse leaped out at me.

But I realized that this may have been a slip of the eye or something. In fact, I probably wouldn't have given it another thought. But then it happened again. I believe it was around a year later or so when I was reading in that same chapter. I had forgotten all about that previous experience. Once again, when I got to the fifty-eighth verse, it leaped out at me.

Therefore, my brothers, stand firm. Let nothing move you. Always give yourselves fully to the work of the Lord, because you know that your labor in the Lord is not in vain.

This verse revealed four areas in my life where I was weak. In fact, I was weak in these areas for the next two decades of my Christian life. God was saying to me in this verse, "Ricky, be steady, be immovable, always abound, and give yourself much to the work of the Lord and know that your work in the Lord is not in vain."

But for many years, I bucked against God's command and did the direct opposite. I was unsteady. I was easily moved from what I was supposed to be doing, and I did not give myself much to the work of the Lord.

You see, it was easy for me to stay confined in my room, studying what it's all about and experiencing God's presence, but when it came to living life in the real world and rubbing shoulders with the people of this world, I had a problem.

I called Jesus my Lord, which means "Supreme Ruler" or "Boss." But I didn't submit to His lordship as well as I should. There were certain things He commanded that took me a long time to obey, such as "Love your enemies, bless them that curse you, do good to them that hate you, and pray for them which despitefully use you or persecute you" (Matthew 5:44).

For many of the beginning years of my Christian life, I got into it with my enemies. I argued with my enemies. I had a hard time trying to make it through a whole year without beating up an enemy. Well, to be honest with you, I beat a few up along the way, and sometimes it wasn't an enemy. It was a fellow Christian.

The Key to Triumphant Christian Living

Jesus promised stability and firm footing in this life's journey for those who not only hear His words but also would act on them. He said,

> Therefore, everyone who hears these words of Mine and acts on them, may be compared to a wise man who built his house upon a rock. And the rain fell, and the floods came, and the winds blew and slammed against that house and it did not fall, for it had been founded on that rock. Everyone who hears these words of Mine and does not act on them, will be like a foolish man who built his house on the sand. The rain fell, and the floods came, and the winds blew and slammed against that house; and it fell—and great was the fall of it.
>
> Matthew 7:24–27

God has provided everything we need for triumphant Christian living. Spiritual strength and development come through the regular practice of prayer, reading the Bible, going to Church, and of being a doer of God's Word.

But I had a problem. When I would allow the enemy to tempt me into sin, many times I would become discouraged. I would slack off on those things that would help me to be strong, and as a result, I would enter a state of spiritual weakness.

The consequence of not submitting my life to the will of God and the words of Jesus were instability. There I was, running wild with my life. I lived an in-and-out, up-and-down, wishy-washy Christian life. I considered myself to be a backsliding veteran.

The Holy Spirit and the Law of Forgiveness

But then I had an experience that helped to slow down this process. The habit in my life was to get up early enough before work to pray and study the Bible. One particular night, I set my alarm clock to get myself up early, but from the time I set the alarm clock to the time I went to bed, I believe I had sinned, and I felt bad about it. I felt like, who am I to get up early and spend time with God? I'm too unworthy to spend time with

God. So, I figured that when the alarm clock goes off in the morning, I'll just shut it off and go back to bed if I want to.

But later the next morning, when the alarm clock went off, something happened when I turned it off. I heard the Holy Spirit inside me say in very clear and distinct words, "When the devil has knocked you down, when the devil has wounded you, this is no time to retreat. This is the time to go to the one who can bind up your wounds!"

As I said previously, when the Holy Spirit speaks to an individual, He does not say things that contradict the Bible. He will always say things that will agree with God's Word. I didn't find out till years later that the Bible teaches that when His people sin, He likens that unto being wounded by the enemy, and God is the one who is willing and ready to bind up and heal our wounds (Isaiah 1:6; Psalm 38:4–6; Jeremiah 30:17).

So what do we do when the enemy gets us to sin? What do we do when we yield to the temptations that the enemy sends along our pathway? Obviously, God knew that we would blow it from time to time; therefore, He gave Christians a law of forgiveness.

The Bible tells us, "If we confess our sins, He is faithful and righteous to forgive us our sins and to cleanse us from all unrighteousness" (1 John 1:9).

This is a partnership covenant we have with God. Our part in this law of forgiveness is to confess our sins to God—whatever that sin is—and then God does His part. He does two things—forgives us of our sins and cleanses us from all unrighteousness.

When Satan manages to get a Christian to sin—when he wounds them, his intention is for that Christian to give up. His goal is for that Christian to stay down, to retreat, to feel unworthy, and to perhaps backslide.

There are two things that kept getting me back on my feet—my knowledge that God's forgiveness is perfect and my desire to continue in my study of God's Word. I knew that my continual investigation in finding out what it's all about would reveal how to win the game of life.

The Third Witness

I eventually began settling down and became more committed to living the Christian life. But what about those experiences I had when I was just a youth? Does God still want to use me after I lived such an uncommitted life for so many years?

The Bible tells us that the gifts and callings of God are without repentance. In other words, when God calls an individual to do a particular thing, He does not change His mind. We may get out of line and cause a delay in the process, but God stands firm in His decision.

Then on April 10, 2002, God sent the third witness and reminded me of my calling. At church this evening, Pastor Tim Bagwell from Lone Tree, Colorado, was our guest speaker.

After Pastor Bagwell completed his sermon, the Holy Spirit began speaking to him about a man who was sitting in the fourth row. That man happened to be me. He called me out in front of the hundreds who were in attendance, "Middle section, fourth row. You're in a black-and-white golf shirt, and you have a beard. Come up here. You want this."

This man doesn't know me. What does he want to talk to me about?

So, I walked to the front and stood before him, and he said, "Let me explain something. God is getting ready to absolutely do something in you because you have a date with destiny. I don't have to say certain things to you. Prophecy knows what has already been said. I'm here to remind you of some things God said to you a long time ago.

"I'm here to say to you, you stand behind a barrier that doesn't seem like it wants to move. But God has a purpose for you in life. God appointed you to have an anointing over your life.

"There was a day when you really didn't understand who you were, and there was something running wild about you. There was a day that in running wild, you got more and more discouraged. Then you got angry, and then you got bitter. Then God started bringing you back around. But you still have that bucking thing about you. Sometimes you just have to buck a little bit. You know, that's all right because God has a lot of spunk on the inside of you. But be cautious, son, because if you will stay under what God has put you under, the things that God spoke to you about in the youth of your walk with Him are going to be fulfilled, and they are going to be manifest."

Then Pastor Bagwell said, "God has placed a pro-claiming anointing upon your life."

The Proclaiming Anointing

When Pastor Bagwell used the word *proclaiming*, I figured that it meant preaching. So, without doing a study of the word proclaim, I automatically thought that I was going to have to stand behind a pulpit in church and deliver messages.

I found out years earlier that every one of us is created by God with a purpose in mind. The only reason you are breathing at this moment is because God desired for you to be here, and He has a plan for your life.

So how does an individual find his or her purpose? The Bible tells us that God works in us to will and to do of His good pleasure (Philippians 2:13). In other words, for us to do our particular purpose in life, God places the desire within us to do it. Whatever you have a passion for is usually a clue as to what you have been called to do. And whatever your purpose is will be used to benefit the lives of others.

It didn't take me long to find out what my passion was. From the time I began my journey with the Lord in September of 1980, I had a strong desire to continue making further advancement in discovering what the God journey is all about. This desire has not left me to this very day.

Another way to find your purpose is by locating your talent. Pastor Keith Moore tells about the time when he was a young child in school. He could speak and perform without any notes, and he could play musical instruments without any formal training in music.

When he reached his adult years, he began preaching. Often without notes, verses of the Bible and illustrations would flow through him. He would sing and play musical instruments. He had the ability to perform without any apparent effort. It all seemed second nature to him. He thought it was all due to his natural talents.

But to be on the safe side, Pastor Moore prayed, "Lord, I don't want to be deceived. I don't want to think something is in me if it's really You. I don't want to neglect giving You thanks and acknowledging what You are and what You are doing in me and through me. I want to see what I am and what You are. Please show me."

Keith sincerely wanted to know what to give God credit for and what to take credit for himself. But he wasn't prepared for what happened next.

The following day, after he prayed this prayer, it seemed as if the grace of God for his life and ministry was suspended from him. God showed him what it would be like if He lifted every grace off him.

Keith said that he couldn't think of a single scripture. He couldn't sing or play a note or remember one word of a single song. He was scheduled to teach the Bible somewhere, and he tried to plan on what he was going to teach, but he finally had to get somebody else to take his place.

He just sat in his office, looking out the window and feeling like an empty bottle. For three days and three nights, he was in such a state that he couldn't do anything. He said the devil kept whispering to him, "You'll never preach again," and he said it felt like he might be right.

But after three days, the grace came back. Keith said, "You'll never hear me say again that anything I do is just a natural talent. When I get up and preach and sing, and when it seems as if scriptures and songs and illustrations just flow out of me effortlessly and naturally, I know, without any doubt, that it's due to the grace of God and not just my own abilities."

Every gift, grace, talent, and skill that people have on the face of this earth came from God, and He should always get the glory for it.

This experience by Keith Moore helped me realize that I not only had the passion to find out what it's all about, but I also had the ability to share it with others. My desire, plus my ability, revealed my calling—sharing with others what it's all about.

So when the Holy Spirit revealed to Pastor Tim Bagwell that there was a proclaiming anointing residing on my life, I figured that I was going to have to preach, and the idea of delivering sermons in front of an assembly of people bothered me.

I am normally a quiet type of person who keeps to himself. When my wife and I began going out together, she would refer to me as a hermit at times. A hermit is one who likes to be alone, far from people—sometimes because of his or her religious beliefs or maybe because he or she simply wants some privacy.

I am a thinker—one who thinks deeply and seriously. I would rather think than talk. I very seldom visit relatives and friends. My mother reminds me from time to time what her address is. I remember when my parents lived a couple of roads over from me, and when I didn't visit them for six weeks or so, my dad came over and said to me, "You are dishonoring your parents!"

At times, I will attend a funeral when one of my relatives die, and it was during one of those visits when my Aunt Karen from Mississippi (where, it seems, most of my relatives live) said to me, "Ricky, you have divorced your family!"

Needless to say, I have some things to work on. I am very content with being quiet and with being by myself. So again, this whole idea of preaching in church bothered me. My wife and son talk more than me.

About five years after this encounter with Pastor Bagwell, I wrote my first book entitled *What It's All About.* As I was writing my second book, *Doing the Will of the Father*, the thought came to me to study the definition of the word proclaim. I looked in Webster's Dictionary and found that the word proclaim means "to declare publicly in either speech or by writing."

Then I looked up the word in my thesaurus, and it said that it means "to publish." Then I looked up the word publish, and it meant "to proclaim." After I studied this out, I laughed, realizing that I was doing exactly what I am supposed to be doing—following my passion in discovering what the God journey is all about and then simply sharing it with others by publishing my writing!

SECTION TWO

What It's All About

Chapter Six

The Creation of Man

THIS IS THE story of how it all started, paraphrased from Genesis 1. In the beginning, God created the heavens and the earth. The earth was formless and void. It was in complete darkness; water completely covered the earth, and the Spirit of God moved above the watery abyss.

The earth was like a blank canvas—without form and empty. The emptiness is God's canvas, and He is the artist. Out of what seems like a mess, everything goes perfectly to its proper place at the sound of God's voice.

On the first day, God said, "Let there be light," and there was light. God then looked on His work for the first day and saw that it was good.

On the second day, God made the atmosphere. The earth was still covered with water, but now there was a sky above the water.

On the third day, God caused the waters of the earth to be gathered unto one place, and He made the dry land appear. Then He caused the earth to bring forth grass, vegetation, and trees. God then looked on His work for the third day and saw that it was good.

On the fourth day, God said, "Let there be lights in the expanse of the heavens to separate the day from the night. Let them be for signs, seasons, days, and years." God then looked on His work for the fourth day and saw that it was good.

On the fifth day, God created every living creature of the waters and every kind of bird to fly above the earth. God then looked on His work for the fifth day and saw that it was good.

On the sixth day, God created the first man, whom He called Adam. Then He made the beasts, animals, and creeping things of the earth, and then He made the first woman, whom Adam called Eve. God then looked on His work for the sixth day and saw that it was good.

God then rested on the seventh day. The number seven in the Bible is a symbol of perfection and completion.

This was now a perfect world for His children. It was a world where there was no such thing as sin, sickness, or death. He created His children to live forever in a completely healthy body and to be surrounded by a world where all their needs would be provided for.

When creating the first man, Adam, The Bible says, "The Lord God formed man of the dust of the ground and breathed into His nostrils the breath of life; and man became a living soul" (Genesis. 2:7).

The natural, physical body that God gave to Adam came from this natural, physical world. It came from the earth. Scientists in the twentieth century finally found out that our physical body has the same chemical element as the dust of the ground. But the real person inside the body came from the inside of God. It was that breath that God breathed into the nostrils of the body made from dust.

God is a spirit, and every one of us as human beings is created in the image and likeness of God. This means that we were created in the spiritual image of God. We are spirit beings living inside this body of flesh, bone, and muscle.

The Trichotomy of Man

Man is a trichotomy. He is a three-part being. We are spirit beings created in the image and likeness of God. We have a soul, which consists of our mind, will, and emotions. And our spirit and soul live inside this natural, physical body.

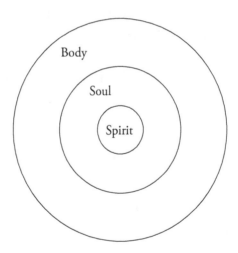

Since Adam's spirit came from the inside of God, it was absorbed with the nature of God. It was God's desire for His children to produce a world full of people who were in His image and likeness.

Therefore, God set a law into motion, which some have called the law of Genesis or the law of beginnings, which says that everything is to produce after their own kind. Every living creature of the waters was to produce after its own kind, vegetation was to produce after its own kind, beasts, animals, and the creeping things of the earth were to produce their own kind, and human beings were to produce after their own kind—the image and likeness of God.

So Why Are We Here?

Why did God create us? Why did He make the earth and us along with it? It wasn't because He needed us. The Bible declares, "The God who made the world and everything in it…is not served by human hands, as if He needed anything" (Acts 17:24–25).

God loves us, but this is not the same as needing us. He did not create human beings because He needed them. As God, He needs nothing. He never felt loneliness in the past or present, and He was not looking for a "friend." If we had never existed, God would still be God—the Unchanging One. He was never dissatisfied with His own eternal existence. When God made the universe, He did what pleased Himself, and since God is perfect, His action was perfect.

Although God did not need us, out of His great love, He chose to create us anyway. Because of God's love and His wonderful creativity, He made us so we can enjoy all that He is and all that He has done.

The Bible tells us that we were created for God's pleasure. We were created by Him and for Him. God created us for His pleasure so that we, as His creation, would have the pleasure of knowing Him.

Although we were created for God's pleasure, this does not mean that human beings were made to entertain God or provide Him with amusement. God is a creative being, and it gives Him pleasure to create. He is also a personal being, and it gives Him pleasure to have other beings whom He can have a genuine relationship with.

We were created in the image and likeness of God, and therefore, we, as human beings, can know God and, therefore, love Him, worship Him, serve Him, and fellowship with Him.

Chapter Seven

The Angelic Realm

LONG AGO, AND before this world ever existed, God created the angels. In fact, the Bible describes the angels singing together and shouting for joy—worshipping God as He was creating this world.

God created the angels before the foundation of this world, which puts this event outside of time itself. Time and space are characteristics of our world, not God's. So, although the Bible does not say specifically when God created the angels, it was sometime before the world was created. Whether this was a day before or billions of years before—again, as we reckon time—we cannot be sure.

While we don't know a whole lot about what was going on during this historical period before the creation of man, there is something that God did want us to know. Out of all the angels that God created, there was one angel who seemed to shine the brightest. He was a leading angel—a special kind of an angel known as a cherub.

God created this angel and brought him into existence and named him Lucifer. This name means "bright one, shining one." God created Lucifer as a very special angel and gave him a very special position.

Lucifer was perfectly beautiful. He was full of wisdom, very skillful, and wise. He was adorned with every precious stone: ruby, topaz, emerald, chrysolite, onyx, jasper, sapphire, turquoise, and beryl. His settings and mountings were of gold.

The workmanship of *tabrets* and pipes were prepared in Lucifer, which the Bible refers to as musical instruments. *Tabrets* (spelled *taborets* in modern English) are small drums like those used to beat out timing for a fife player. Pipes probably refer to tubes used to produce tones by blowing air through them, as in an organ. This seems to tell us that Lucifer had the makings of percussion instruments and wind instruments built into his very being. One of the functions of angels is to worship God around His throne, and the Bible seems to indicate that Lucifer would lead angels in worship, and that music—beautiful music—was intrinsic to him.

Lucifer was perfect in his ways from the very beginning when God created him. He was obedient to all the laws that God gave him to live by. We don't know how long Lucifer was obedient to God—but later, something went very, very wrong with Lucifer.

Iniquity was found in him. Iniquity refers to "wickedness, perverseness, and unrighteousness." Lucifer originated a thing called sin. He became a selfish being. His eyes were focused on himself and on how beautiful he was. He was lifted in pride, and his sinful desire now was to be God. He had such persuasive power that he managed to persuade one-third of all of God's angels to join him in his effort to dethrone God.

Lucifer said in his heart,

> I will ascend into heaven, I will exalt
> my throne above the stars of God: I
> will sit also upon the mount of the

congregation, in the sides of the north:
I will ascend above the heights of the
clouds; I will be like the Most High.

Isaiah 14:13–14

When Lucifer finally went for it, he didn't even get to first base. He was cast out of heaven. Lucifer became who we now know as Satan, the devil. Jesus said, "I saw Satan fall from heaven like lightning" (Luke 10:18).

Going back to when God made the heavens and the earth in six days, look at something very strange. When God completed His work for the first day, He saw that it was good. He said the same thing in days three through six. But after He completed His work for the second day, He did not say, "It is good." After God made the atmosphere in the second day, what was it in the atmosphere that influenced Him not to say, "It is good"?

The Bible tells us that Satan is the prince of the power of the air. One of the dwelling places of Satan and his demon spirits is in the atmosphere of this earth.

Where did demons come from? One-third of all of God's angels chose to listen to the voice of Satan and, as a result, joined him. They became Satan's demon spirits.

Hell was created for Satan and his demon spirits. Hell is a place of torment. It was created as an eternal jail for spirits who are on Satan's side of the line. But their appointed time had not yet come.

Chapter Eight

The Fall of Man

BEFORE GOD CONTINUED in His eternal plan for His children, there was a test that they had to pass. God planted a garden eastward in Eden and said, "Out of all these trees in the garden, you can freely eat of all, except for this tree in the middle of the garden. Don't eat of that one" (author's paraphrase).

God lost one-third of his angels to Lucifer because they chose to listen to his voice. This test in the garden was a test to see whose voice His children would listen to. God knew that the very tree He commanded his children not to eat from would be the very tree that Satan would tempt God's children with. Then one day, the test began. Satan said, "Did God tell you not to eat of that tree? God is holding out on you. He knows that if you eat of that tree, you're going to be like gods, knowing good and evil" (author's paraphrase).

As history tells us, God's children chose to listen to the voice of Satan rather than God. God lost one-third of His angels to Satan, and now He lost his children. The Bible teaches us that you become the servant to who you obey or to whoever you yield yourself to (Rom. 6:16).

Then somehow, someway, the dominion that God had given Adam over this natural, physical world was transferred into the hands of Satan, and he now became the god of this world.

God originally created everything to be a blessing to mankind, but when Satan took over, he started twisting things into their opposite or perverted direction for them now to become a curse to mankind.

No longer would His children live forever in their physical body. Now the aging process would begin, and man would eventually get old and die.

No longer would man experience a completely healthy body. Now man would experience sickness and disease.

No longer did the earth produce only pure vegetation. Now weeds began growing out of the ground.

The list could go on and on concerning the tragic changes that took place when Satan took over as the god of this world system.

Sin Nature

The most tragic thing that took place was when Satan's sin nature was now lodged into the spirit of mankind.

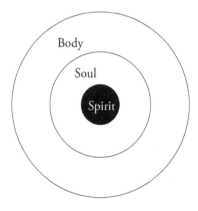

God—along with His nature that was within man's spirit—was separated from man, and now Satan became the illegitimate stepfather of mankind.

Because of the law of Genesis that says everything is to produce after its own kind, mankind is now producing a world full of people whose spirits are absorbed with the nature of Satan.

Hell was not originally prepared for mankind. It was originally prepared for Satan and his demon spirits. But now since mankind is born into this world with Satan's sin nature lodged in their spirit, they receive the same spiritual judgment as their illegitimate stepfather—hell for an eternal home!

In order to get a better understanding of this sin nature that we are born with, let's take a look again at what Lucifer said when he was planning to take over God's throne, and pay close attention to how many times he uses the word I:

> I will ascend into Heaven, I will exalt my throne above the stars of God: I will sit upon the mount of the congregation, in the sides of the north: I will ascend above the heights of the clouds; I will be like the Most High.
>
> Isaiah 14:13–14

Sin nature is a selfish nature that says, "I am my own god. I call the shots for my life. Whether it is right or wrong, I think how I want to think. I talk how I want to talk. I act how I want to act. I am my own boss."

After Satan took over as god of this world system and millions of people had now occupied the earth, they didn't know they had a sin nature inside of them. They naturally sinned because it was their nature to sin. There were no laws set up that told them what was right and what was wrong.

So, God raised up a man by the name of Moses and gave him the law of the Ten Commandments. The Ten Commandments helped people realize what sin was. They found out that they were breaking every one of God's laws and were now guilty before God.

Perhaps you are reading this, and you consider yourself to be a good person. You might even think of some things that might qualify you to be a good person. But the major question is this: Do you think God would consider you to be a good person?

Let me ask you a few questions using God's commandments to see where you stand with God. (I assume that your answer is yes to the following questions because most of us have broken these commandments.)

Have you ever told a lie? I don't care if it's a so-called white lie, half-truth, or stretching the truth. It is still a lie. Have you done this?

What does that make you?

A liar.

Have you ever stolen anything? It doesn't have to be a big thing. It could even be somebody else's pen or even a paper clip off somebody else's desk at work or at school. Have you done this?

What does that make you?

A thief.

Have you ever used God's name in vain or perhaps used it as a cussword? This is what the Bible calls blasphemy. It is a very serious sin in the sight of God. Have you done this?

Have you ever committed adultery?

Jesus taught us that if you even look at another individual with lust, you have already committed adultery with that individual in your heart. Have you done this?

If your answer is yes to breaking these commandments, in God's sight and by your own admission, you are a lying, thieving, blaspheming adulterer of heart, and that's only four of God's Ten Commandments.

The Bible tells us, "All liars will have their part in the lake of fire. No thief, blasphemer, adulterer, or fornicator will enter God's kingdom."

The Bible also tells us that it is appointed unto mankind once to die, but after this comes the Judgment. When you stand before God on Judgment Day, and since you have broken God's laws all those times, will you go to heaven? Or will you go to hell?

If you are honest, most likely, you will say "hell." But I have good news for you. Somebody paid your fine!

Repentance and faith in Christ are what cause a person to receive forgiveness of their sins. It's simply saying to God with a sincere heart, "God, I come to you as a sinner. I have broken Your commandments. Please forgive me. Jesus, come into my life. I receive You as my Lord and Savior."

The word repent is a military word that means "about face." In other words, a person who has chosen to cross over onto God's side of the line is one who has chosen to turn his or her back on sin and put his or her trust in Jesus.

Chapter Nine

God's Master Plan Of Redemption

THE BIBLE DESCRIBES the appearance of God as a fire from the loins up and from the loins down. In other words, He is illuminated with glorious light.

When God created His first two children, Adam and Eve, the Bible tells us that they were crowned with God's glory. The word crowned means "to circle about." They were surrounded and clothed with glorious light.

But when they sinned, they fell short of this glory. The light was put out, and they realized that they were naked. They sewed fig leaves together and made themselves aprons to cover their nakedness.

Then God does something that gives us the first glimpse of what He was about to do to buy mankind and this world back to him. For the first time, an innocent animal was killed in order to clothe the nakedness of Adam and Eve. Because of their sin, an innocent animal was killed in order to cover them.

We now see a symbol of what God was about to do. God raised up a priesthood. He had them go through various ceremonies until they finally qualified to offer up sacrifices for the people.

The priest would take an innocent animal such as a lamb. He would lay his hands on this animal, and somehow, someway, God caused the sins of the people to go into this lamb. Although the lamb never committed a sin, the lamb became sin for the people. The lamb was then sacrificed, and the people's sins were covered. But the sacrifice of animals was not a perfect sacrifice. It could only forgive them for the sins that they had committed. The sin nature that was lodged in their spirits could not be removed by the blood of animals.

As a result, they went back to habitual sinning because sin was their nature. If you take a pig out of the mud and clean him up, he will go right back to it because his nature is to wallow in mud.

Therefore, after a while, their sins would become full again, and the sacrifice of animals would have to be repeated. This was an Old Testament practice. The Old Testament was never meant to be permanent. It was only temporary until the perfect sacrifice would show up on the scene and then would begin the new and final testament.

Throughout the Old Testament, it was prophesied that God was sending the Savior. The Savior was the one who would buy mankind and the world back to God. But for this person to qualify to be the Savior, He must meet certain unique specifications.

When God created the first man, Adam, He created him to be able to withstand temptation from the enemy. Adam had the authority to overcome. But Adam willingly fell into the hands of the enemy.

Although God was not responsible for Adam's fall, God did create the man that fell. Also, since mankind was the key to the fall, man was going to have to be the key to the redemption.

Therefore, this person who was to come must be unique in order for Him to qualify as Savior. This savior had to be both 100 percent God and 100 percent man.

Jesus, the Savior

In the Old Testament, it was prophesied, "Behold a virgin shall conceive, and bear a Son, and shall call His name Immanuel" (Isaiah 7:14). The name Immanuel means "God with us."

Then we find the manifestation of this prophecy in the New Testament.

> Now in the sixth month, the angel Gabriel was sent from God to a city in Galilee called Nazareth, to a virgin engaged to a man whose name was Joseph, of the descendants of David; and the virgin's name was Mary. And coming in, he said to her, "Greetings, favored one! The Lord is with you." But she was very perplexed at this statement and kept pondering what kind of salutation this was.

The angel said to her, "Do not be afraid, Mary; for you have found favor with God. And behold you will conceive in your womb and bear a Son, and you shall name Him Jesus. He will be great and will be called the Son of the Most High; and the Lord God will give Him the throne of His father David; and He will reign over the house of Jacob forever, and His kingdom will have no end."

Mary said to the angel, "How can this be, since I am a virgin?"

The angel answered and said to her, "The Holy Spirit will come upon you, and the power of the Most High will overshadow you; and for that reason the Holy Child shall be called the Son of God."

Luke 1:26–35

Now the birth of Jesus Christ was as follows: when His mother Mary had been betrothed to Joseph, before they came together, she was found to be with child by the Holy Spirit. And Joseph, her husband, being a righteous man and not wanting to disgrace her, planned to send her away secretly. But when he had considered this, behold, an angel of the Lord appeared to him in a dream, saying, "Joseph, son of David, do not be afraid to take Mary as your wife; for the Child who has been conceived in her is of the Holy Spirit. She will bear a Son; and you shall call His name Jesus, for He will save His people from their sins."

Matthew 1:18–21

Mary Had a Little Lamb

Why did Jesus have to be born through a virgin? So that He would be born into this world without Satan's sin nature. If He entered this world with sin in His spirit, He would be guilty like everyone else, and He would not qualify as the innocent lamb who would take away the sin of the world.

About thirty years later, God revealed to the prophet, John, the Baptist, who Jesus was. John then looked at Jesus and said, "*Behold the Lamb of God, who takes away the sin of the world!*" (John 1:29).

The Bible Calls Jesus God

God, the Father says of His Son, "*Your throne, O God, is forever and ever*" (Hebrews 1:8).

The Bible tells us, "*God was manifest in the flesh*" (1 Timothy 3:16).

In the first chapter of the Gospel of John, the Bible refers to Jesus as the Word:

> "*And the Word was made flesh, and dwelt among us, (and we beheld His glory, the glory as of the only begotten of the Father,) full of grace and truth*" (John 1:14)

Keeping in mind that the Word is referring to Jesus, look at the underlined words in the first three verses of this chapter:

In the beginning was <u>the Word</u>, and <u>the Word</u> was with God, and <u>the Word</u> was God. <u>The same</u> was in the beginning with God. All things were made by <u>Him:</u> And without <u>Him</u> was not anything made that was made. (John 1:1–3)

By putting the name of Jesus in place of the underlined words, it makes it even clearer:

In the beginning was Jesus, and Jesus was with God, and Jesus was God.

Jesus was in the beginning with God. All things were made by Jesus: And without Jesus was not anything made that was made.

Scripture also declares, "*God created all things by Jesus Christ*" (Ephesians 3:9).

For by Him were all things created, that are in heaven, and that are in earth, visible and invisible, whether they be thrones, or dominions, or principalities, or powers: all things were created by him, and for him.

Colossians 1:16

It was Jesus Himself, the creator of all things, who came to the rescue of His creation. Jesus was 100 percent God, 100 percent man, and the innocent Lamb of God who came to take away the sin of the world.

Chapter Ten

Jesus Paid The Price

AFTER GOD CREATED the first man, Adam, He placed him in the Garden of Eden and gave him a test. As history tells us, Adam failed that test. He chose to listen to the voice of Satan instead of God. As a result, sin nature entered man, and God separated from humanity.

Jesus, the Last Adam

The Bible calls Jesus as *the last Adam*. Jesus, the last Adam, came to reverse what the first Adam caused in the Garden of Eden. Jesus came with a solution for the sin nature that was lodged in the human spirit.

But before He was able to provide this solution, He must first pass the test that Adam failed. Whose voice will Jesus listen to.

Then one day, the test began.

> Jesus was led by the Holy Spirit into the wilderness, where He fasted for forty days and forty nights. The tempter then appeared on the scene and said, "If you are God's Son, command these stones to be made loaves of bread."
>
> Jesus replied, "It has been written, Man shall not live by bread alone, but by every Word that comes forth from the mouth of God."
>
> Then the devil took Him into the Holy City and placed Him on a turret of the temple sanctuary and said to Him, "If you are the Son of God, throw yourself down; for it is written, He will give His angels charge over you, and they will bear you up on

their hands, lest you strike your foot against a stone."

Jesus said to him, "On the other hand, it is written also, you shall not tempt the Lord your God."

Again, the devil took Him on a very high mountain and showed Him all the kingdoms of the world and the magnificence of them, and he said to him, "These things, all taken together, I will give You, if You will prostrate yourself before me and worship me."

Then Jesus said to him, "Begone, Satan! For it has been written, you shall worship the Lord your God, and Him alone shall you serve."

Then the devil departed from him, and behold, angels came and ministered to Him.

Matthew 4:1–11

The Solution for Sin Nature

Jesus came to provide the solution for the sin nature that was lodged in man's spirit. Your spirit must be born again!

> There was a man of the Pharisees named Nicodemus, a ruler of the Jews; this man came to Jesus by night and said to Him, "Rabbi, we know that you have come from God as a teacher; for no one can do these signs that you do unless God is with him." Jesus answered and said to him, "Truly, I say to you, unless one is born again, he cannot see the kingdom of God."
>
> Nicodemus said to Him, "How can a man be born when he is old? He cannot enter a second time into his mother's womb and be born, can he?"
>
> Jesus answered, "Truly, truly, I say to you, unless one is born of water and the Spirit, he cannot enter into the Kingdom of God. That which is

born of flesh is flesh, and that which is born of the Spirit is spirit."

"Do not be amazed that I said to you, you must be born again. The wind blows where it wishes and you hear the sound of it, but do not know where it comes from and where it is going, so is everyone who is born of the Spirit."

John 3:1–8

Jesus didn't leave Nicodemus hanging as to how a person becomes born again spiritually. He said to Nicodemus, "For God so loved the world, that He gave His only begotten Son, that whoever believes in Him shall not perish but have eternal life" (John 3:16).

The word *believe* comes from a Greek word that means "to trust in, cling to and rely on."

A person who believes in Jesus is one who has chosen to put his trust in Him, cling to Him, and rely on Him. This kind of believing is what produces the new birth. The Bible declares, "Whoever believes that Jesus is the Christ is born of God" (1 John 5:1).

Jesus Pays the Price

For the new birth to become a reality in an individual's life, Jesus must pay the ultimate price. He was the only one who was qualified to purchase man's salvation.

The night before the crucifixion, Jesus finished serving communion to his disciples in the upper room and then went to the garden of Gethsemane to pray.

Knowing that the cross and the grave were before Him, Jesus felt a need to spend time in intercession so He might have the strength needed to face what lay before Him.

The mental and spiritual battle Jesus was experiencing that night was intense. In fact, the Bible tells us, "And being in agony, He prayed more earnestly: and His sweat was as it were great drops of blood falling down to the ground" (Luke 22:44). Sweating blood is a medical condition called hematidrosis—a condition that occurs only in individuals who are in a highly emotional state.

Then God provided supernatural assistance. There appeared an angel unto Him from heaven, strengthening Him. This angel imparted strength, empowered, and recharged Jesus, renewing his vitality with the strength needed to victoriously face the most difficult hour in His life! After being supercharged, Jesus was ready to face the cross.

The Roman soldiers showed up on the scene in the garden to arrest Jesus. Jesus then stepped forward and asked, "Whom are you seeking?" They answered Him, "Jesus of Nazareth." Jesus said, "I am He."

These mighty words, "I am He," come from the Greek words *ego eimi*, which is more accurately translated as "I Am!" This was not the first time that Jesus used this phrase to identify Himself; He also used it in other places so that when the hearers of that day heard those words, *ego eimi*, they immediately recognized them as the very words God used to identify Himself when He spoke to Moses on Mount Horeb.

When God raised up this man, Moses, to free the Israelites from Egyptian bondage, Moses asked God,

> Behold, when I come to the children of Israel, and shall say unto them, The God of your fathers has sent me unto you; and they shall say to me, what is His name? What shall I say to them?"

And God said unto Moses, "I Am
who I Am and what I Am, and I will
be what I will be. You shall say this to
the Israelites: I Am has sent me to you!

Exodus 3:13–14

When Jesus revealed Himself to these soldiers that He was the great "I Am," these three hundred to six hundred soldiers fell backward to the ground. The original Greek scriptures from where these words come from teaches us that these soldiers staggered and stumbled backward as if some force had hit them and pushed them backward, and they fell so hard, it appeared that they fell dead or fell like a corpse.

The members of this militia that came to arrest Jesus were knocked flat by some kind of force! After Jesus proved that He couldn't be taken by force, He willfully surrendered to them, knowing that it was all a part of the Father's plan for the redemption of mankind.

The Bible tells us, "They that had laid hold on Jesus led Him away to Caiaphas the high priest, where the scribes and the elders were assembled" (Matthew 26:57).

These words ("led Him away") come from the Greek word *apago*—the same word used to depict a shepherd who ties a rope about the neck of his sheep and then leads it down the path to where it needs to go.

Jesus wasn't gagged and dragged to the high priest as one who was putting up a fight or resisting arrest. Instead, the Greek word *apago* plainly tells us that the soldiers lightly slipped a rope about Jesus's neck and led Him down the path as He followed behind, just like a sheep being led by a shepherd. The Old Testament prophesied that he would be led as a sheep to the slaughter.

He then yielded to their excruciating punishment. They began spitting on His face; and after spitting on His face, they doubled their fists and whacked Him violently on the face! They blindfolded him and continued to hit Him while they mocked Him.

Then Jesus went through the scourging process. He was stripped completely naked so his entire flesh would be open and uncovered to the beating action of the torturer's whip. He was then tied to the whipping post.

The scourge itself consisted of a short wooden handle with several eighteen- to twenty-four-inch-long straps of leather protruding from it. The ends of these pieces of leather were equipped with sharp, rugged pieces of metal, wire, glass, and jagged fragments of bone. This was one of the most feared and deadly weapons of the Roman world.

Jesus's physical body was severely disfigured by the slashing blows of this kind of whip. In fact, it was marred nearly beyond recognition.

Then when this scourging process was concluded, Jesus was delivered to be crucified. The cross beam, normally weighing about one hundred pounds, was carried on the back of Jesus. When He could no longer carry it alone, a man named Simon was forced to help Him.

Once they arrived at the crucifixion site, they nailed Jesus to the cross. When Jesus was nailed to the cross, the nails were not driven through the palms of His hands but through his wrists. Once the wrists were secured in place, the feet came next. His legs were positioned so that His feet pointed downward, with the soles pressed against the post on which He was suspended. A long nail was then driven between the bones of His feet into the vertical beam.

When the cross beam was dropped into the groove, Jesus suffered excruciating pain as His hands and wrists were wrenched by the sudden jerking motion.

For Jesus to breathe, He had to push Himself up by His feet. However, because the pressure on His feet became unbearable, it wasn't possible for Him to remain long in this position; so, eventually, He would collapse back into the hanging position.

When he was finally too exhausted and could no longer push Himself upward on the nail lodged in his feet, the process of asphyxiation began.

Due to the extreme loss of blood and hyperventilation, Jesus began to experience severe dehydration. After several hours of this torment, Jesus's heart began to fail. His lungs collapsed, and excess fluids began filling the lining of His heart and lungs, adding to this slow process of asphyxiation.

Jesus's final words were "It is finished."

SECTION THREE

The Great Beyond

Chapter Eleven

The Resurrection

BEFORE JESUS WENT to the cross, He warned His disciples of what He was about to go through.

> Behold, we go up to Jerusalem, and all things that are written by the proph- ets concerning the Son of man shall be accomplished. For He shall be delivered unto the Gentiles, and shall be mocked, and spitefully entreated, and spit upon; and they shall scourge Him, and put Him to death: and the third day He shall rise again.
>
> Luke 18:31–33

When Jesus was nailed to the cross, two criminals were also nailed on the cross with Him, one on His right hand and the other on His left. One of the men believed in Jesus and said to Him, "Lord, remember me when You come into Your Kingdom." Jesus said to him, "Today, you will be with Me in Paradise" (Luke 23:42–43).

Jesus was about to die on the cross and would not be resurrected until three days later. How could He tell this man that he would be with Him in paradise that day?

Death

The word *death* in the Bible means "separation." There are three kinds of death that the Bible talks about: spiritual death, physical death, and the second death.

Spiritual Death

When God gave Adam the test in the Garden of Eden, He said to him, "Adam, you may eat of all these trees in the garden. But don't eat of this tree over here in the middle of the garden. If you eat of that one, you are going to die that very day" (author's paraphrase).

As history tells us, Adam ate of that forbidden tree, and yet his physical body continued to live on for many years after. God was not talking about a physical death that Adam would die of that day; He was talking about spiritual death. God, along with His nature that Adam's spirit was absorbed with, separated from Adam. As a result, every one of us born into this world was born in spiritual death and separated from a relationship with God.

Physical Death

At the point of physical death, the spirit and soul of an individual separate from the body and are translated to their next eternal destination.

Previously, Jesus talked about a temporary abiding place for people who die. The Old Testament word for "the world of the dead" is "*Sheol*," which appears sixty-five times. The New Testament word is "*Hades*," which appears forty-two times.

The Bible tells us that the location of this world is *down* (Numbers 16:33).

When Jesus died on the cross, He separated from His body and descended into the lower parts of the earth (Ephesians 4:9).

Jesus told His disciples,

> For as Jonah was, for three days and three nights, in the whale's belly, so shall the Son of man be, for three days and three nights, in the heart of the earth.
>
> Matthew 12:40

The word *heart* comes from the Greek word *kardia*, which refers to the middle. While Jesus's physical body was placed in a tomb on the surface or near the surface of the earth, His spirit and soul descended into the center of the earth.

Previously, Jesus talked about this world of the dead when He related the factual record of two men—Abraham and Lazarus—who lived and died. They both went to Hades but not to the same part!

Jesus taught us that there were two compartments: There was a compartment called Abraham's Bosom, also known as paradise, which was a temporary home for the righteous—a place of comfort. Then there was this other compartment, which was a place of torment where all the wicked dead go at the point of physical death. The man whom Jesus spoke of, who went to this compartment, said, "I am tormented in this flame!"

These two compartments were separated by some sort of chasm, a fixed great gulf. This was a chasm that separated the believers from the unbelievers. They could look at one another from the two compartments, but they could not cross over.

Some Bible teachers also believe that this chasm has no bottom to it and that it could very well be the "bottomless pit" into which Satan is cast at the Second Coming of the Lord Jesus Christ.

Before the resurrection of Christ, why didn't believers go right to heaven when they died? Because their spirit was not born again. Jesus said, "Unless a person is born again, he cannot see the kingdom of God…he cannot enter the kingdom of God" (John 3:3–5).

Finally, the price has been paid. When Jesus died on the cross, He descended into Hades and revealed Himself to His people. They then became born again. At the end of three days, Jesus entered back into His body and was raised from the dead.

Before Jesus went back to heaven from where He came from, He liberated the righteous from their captivity in the lower parts of the earth and led these captives to heaven.

Now when a Christian dies, he does not go into the lower parts of the earth to be held captive but goes to heaven to live and await the resurrection of the body.

Chapter Twelve

The Gates Of Hell

AS I SAID earlier in this book, when I was a young teenager, I was afraid of spending eternity in hell. The idea of living forever in fire was terrifying. When you read the following true stories in these next two chapters, keep in mind what we learned in the previous chapter: hell is in the lower parts of the earth.

I met a man years ago who lifted his shirt and showed me the knife wound on his side. He explained to me that after he was stabbed, he died. His spirit separated from his body and started sinking into the earth. He said, "I knew I was going to hell." I met this man only briefly, and I don't even know if he knew what the Bible says concerning the location of hell. But his time was not up yet. He was allowed to come back into his body and continue to live his life.

The Die-hard Atheist

There was one man who was very stubborn when it came to his atheistic beliefs. In fact, he wouldn't let any Christian tell him about God. One day, he ripped a Bible from the hands of a coworker, threw it on the ground, and stomped on it, cursing the man and his Bible. He accused the Christian man of being weak and brainless.

Later, after years of confessed atheism, he suffered severe chest pains. Doctors opened him up for exploratory surgery; they immediately closed him up and told him he had less than twenty-four hours to live.

While he lay on the bed that night, he somehow knew he was about to go out into eternity. He knew he was going to a place where he did not want to end up.

That very night, his heart stopped. He then separated from his body and descended into deep darkness. The darkness was so thick, he felt like he was wearing it.

After descending for what seemed quite some time, he heard the horrifying screams of tormented souls. He was pulled by a strong force right up to the gates of hell.

But his time was not up yet. He was pulled back up into his body and was revived. The next morning, he called for the only Christian man he knew. The Christian then proclaimed the good news of salvation through Jesus Christ. The man then received Jesus Christ as his Lord and Savior.

The Christian then prayed for the man's healing, and as a result, three weeks later, he walked out of the hospital as a walking miracle.

Why is it that when many atheists are on their death-bed, they call for someone who knows God? The Bible tells us that the truth about God is known to mankind instinctively. God has put this knowledge in our hearts.

Kenneth Hagin

When Kenneth Hagin was born, he was born prematurely with a deformed heart, and he weighed less than two pounds. As a young child, he never ran or played like other children. He never had a normal childhood. When he was fifteen years old, he became totally bedridden. Five doctors said that he wouldn't live.

Then finally, one day, he took a turn for the worse. As soon as the clock struck 7:30, his heart stopped beating. Kenneth felt the blood cease to circulate way down at the end of his toes, and they seemed to go numb. This numbness spread from his toes to his feet, ankles, knees, hips, stomach, and his heart; and he leaped out of his body.

When he separated from his body, he never lost consciousness. When he came out of his body, he could see his family in the room, but he couldn't contact them. He wanted to say good-bye to his mother, grandmother, and brother; but he leaped out of his body before he got the chance.

Then he began to descend into the earth. He said it was like descending deep into a well, cavern, or cave. He continued to descend feet first, lower and lower into the earth.

He looked up, and he could see the lights of the earth until they finally faded away. Darkness surrounded him.

The farther down he went, the darker it became and the hotter it became—until, finally, way down beneath him, he could see fingers of light playing on the wall of darkness, and he came to the bottom of the pit. When he came to the bottom of the pit, he saw what caused the fingers of light. In front of him, he saw the gates or the entrance into hell; and he saw giant orange flames with a white crest.

Then he was pulled toward hell just like a magnet pulls metal unto itself. He could feel the heat hitting him in the face, and he knew that once he entered through those gates, he could not come back.

But suddenly, he heard a voice above the blackness and the darkness. It sounded like the voice of a man. He didn't know if it was Jesus or an angel, but it didn't speak in the English language. It was a foreign language. He didn't know who it was, but when He spoke those few words, the place shook.

Then something was pulling him back. He floated from the entrance to hell, and then like a suction from above, he floated up headfirst through the darkness. Before he got to the top, he could see the light. It was like he was in a well and could see the light up above.

When he finally reached the top, he found himself on the porch of the home he lived in. He could see the porch swing. He could see the giant cedar trees in the yard. He stood there for a second, and then he went right through the wall—not through the door or window, through the wall—and seemed to leap inside his body like somebody would slip their foot inside their shoe.

But before he leaped inside his body, he could see his grandmother sitting on the edge of the bed, holding his body in her arms. When he got inside his body, he could communicate with her. He doesn't know how he knew it, but he said to his grandmother, "Granny, I'm going again, and I won't be back."

She said, "Son, I thought you weren't coming back this time."

He said, "Granny, where's Momma? I want to tell her good-bye."

She said, "Son, I told your mother you were gone, and she rushed out the door praying."

Then he heard his mother praying. She was praying at the top of her lungs and could be heard for blocks around.

He said, "Tell Momma I said good-bye! Tell Momma I love her. Tell Momma I appreciate everything she has done for me. Tell Momma that I said if I've ever put a wrinkle on her face or a gray hair on her head, I'm sorry, and I ask her to forgive me."

He then felt himself slipping. He said, "Granny, I'm going again." He kissed her on the cheek and said, "Good-bye."

Kenneth Hagin once again slipped out of his body, and for the second time, he went through the same process, descending into the earth, reaching the bottom and seeing the entrance into hell, hearing the voice from above speaking in a foreign language that caused the whole place to shake.

Then, just as it happened the first time, he was pulled back from the entrance of hell. Once again, he found himself on the surface of the earth as he slipped back into his body. He spoke to his grandmother momentarily, and then for the third time, he slipped out of his body and was descending once more toward hell.

When Kenneth Hagin was nine years old, his Sunday school teacher asked him and the other boys in class, "How many of you want to go to heaven?" Every one of them wanted to go to heaven.

She said, "When the pastor gives the invitation this morning, go down to the front." When the invitation was given, several of them went down to the front. They shook the pastor's hand, joined the church, and were baptized in water.

Kenneth was deceived. Salvation does not come through water baptism or joining a church. Salvation comes through receiving Jesus Christ as your Lord and Savior.

Scripture declares,

> *For God so loved the world, that He gave His only begotten Son, that whoever believes in Him will not perish but have eternal life. If you confess with your mouth that Jesus is Lord and believe in your heart that God raised Him from the dead, you will be saved; for with the heart a person believes, resulting in righteousness, and with the mouth he confesses, resulting in salvation.*
>
> John 3:16, Romans 10:9–10

Kenneth Hagin was deceived. He joined a church and was baptized in water, and he thought that was going to get him into heaven.

So, the third time that he was heading toward hell, he cried out, "God! I belong to the church! I've been baptized in water!" He waited for an answer, but there was no answer, only the echo of his voice through the darkness.

The second time, he cried a little louder, "God! I belong to the church! I've been baptized in water!" Again, he only heard the echo of his voice.

Then he literally screamed, "God! God! I belong to the church! I've been baptized in water!" For the third time, he only heard the echo of his voice.

He reached the bottom of the pit and was pulled toward the entrance into hell. But suddenly, he heard that voice again; the place shook, and he was pulled toward the surface of the earth.

Then by the grace of God, he realized that the only way to be saved was to accept Jesus Christ as his Savior. The Bible tells us that,

> God has given His Son, Jesus, to be the Savior of this world. There is no other name under heaven whereby a person can be saved, except through the name of Jesus Christ.
>
> 1 John 4:14, Acts 4:12

This time, as Kenneth was going up through the darkness, he prayed, "Oh, God! I come to You in the name of the Lord Jesus Christ. I ask You to forgive me for my sins and to cleanse me from all sin."

When he entered his body, his physical voice picked up his prayer right in the middle of the sentence, and he continued to pray. As a result, he received Jesus Christ as his Lord and Savior.

Kenneth managed to live for four more months after this experience. Then four days before his sixteenth birthday, he was dying. He knew all day that he was dying. He had so much experience with death that he knew he was dying.

The temperature got to 106 degrees that day, and they didn't have any air-conditioning back then. But his body was so cold, they wrapped him up in blankets. They got out all the hot water bottles and heated bricks, wrapped them, and put them around him, trying to keep him warm.

Then about 1:30 in the afternoon, death came and fastened itself on him. He said to his little brother, "Run and get Momma—quick! I want to tell her good-bye."

After his brother left the room, the whole room lit up with the glory of God. The whole room filled up with this bright light—brighter than the sun shining on snow. He then went up into that glory. He left his body and ascended.

He looked down into the room and saw his body lying on the bed. His eyes were set, and his mouth was open in death. He ascended to about where the top of the house was.

Then suddenly, he heard a voice speak in the English language, but he didn't see anything. He believed it was Jesus. The voice said, "Go back! Go back! Go back to earth! Your work is not done!"

He then descended and came back down into the room and slipped into his body. One year later, God totally healed him.

God called Kenneth Hagin to preach the gospel. He started preaching as a young teenager. He preached all his life without retiring until he finally went home to be with the Lord in 2003 at eighty-seven years old.

Chapter Thirteen

Beyond The Gates

NO ONE LOVES you more than Jesus. He warned about the judgment and hell more than anyone else. He warned people about hell more than He spoke of heaven. Jesus spoke more about hell than heaven and spent much time warning people not to go there.

So, what would it have been like if Kenneth Hagin did not repent? What would it have been like if he went through the gates of hell?

Bill Wiese

On November 22, 1998, Bill Wiese and his wife, Annette, spent the evening at the home of one of their close friends. They headed home around 11:00 p.m. and went to bed shortly before midnight.

Suddenly, at 3:00 a.m., on the twenty-third, without any notice, Bill found himself being hurled into the air and then falling to the ground, completely out of control.

When he landed, it appeared that he was in some sort of a prison cell. The walls of the cell were made from rough, unsmoothed stone and had a door made from what appeared to be thick metal bars. Bill was not dreaming—he was in this strange place.

Although he was fully awake and aware of his surroundings, he didn't know what was happening, how he got there, or why he was in that place until it was shown and explained to him later during his journey.

The very first thing he noticed was the extreme heat. The temperature was so intense—far beyond anything the human body could tolerate. His flesh should have dissolved from his body, but it didn't. It was so hot that he thought, *why am I still alive? How could I survive such intense heat?*

The severity of this heat took every ounce of strength out of him. This wasn't a bad dream; it was real. Bill didn't realize it yet—but he had fallen into hell.

He was taken there not for being good or bad. The reason he was shown this place was to bring back a message to warn people that hell does exist—it is a real place.

He was in a cell that was approximately fifteen feet high by ten feet wide, with a fifteen-foot depth. The walls seemed to be made of rough stone with rigid bars on the door. He felt as if he was a prisoner who was being held in a temporary holding area, awaiting his final hours before meeting a far more terrifying destiny.

Bill lay on the floor of this cell in total weakness. He lifted his head and began to look around. Immediately, he realized that he wasn't alone. He saw two enormous beasts unlike anything he had ever seen.

Hell was originally created for Satan and his demon spirits. Hell is a place of torment. It was created as an eternal jail for spirits who are on Satan's side of the line.

These creatures that Bill saw were about ten to thirteen feet tall. They were not of this world, and Bill became completely paralyzed with fear when they looked at him with pure, unrestrained hatred. He was in a state of panic and still had no idea where he was.

Bill heard the creatures talking to each other, and although he could not understand the language they spoke, he somehow understood what they were saying. They blasphemed God, used horrible words, expressing their extreme hatred for God.

Suddenly, the creatures turned their attention toward Bill. He wanted to get up and run, but he had absolutely no strength in his body. He was not only physically weak, but he was also mentally and emotionally drained, even though he had been there only for a few minutes.

Then one of the beasts picked him up. He can't explain this, but he somehow knew that the creature holding him had the strength approximately one thousand times greater than man's strength. The beast threw him against the wall, and he fell to the floor. It felt like every bone in his body was broken. But somehow it seemed like the pain was being softened. He knew he didn't feel the full brunt of the pain. Why was the pain being blocked?

Then the second beast grabbed Bill from behind in a bear hug. He felt like a rag doll in its clutches in comparison to his enormous size. These creatures didn't have any respect for the human body. The second creature reached around and plunged his claws into his chest and ripped them outward. His flesh hung from his body like ribbons as he fell again to the cell floor.

Although Bill pleaded for mercy, they had no mercy—absolutely none. They were pure evil. It seemed to heighten their desire to torment him more when he asked for mercy.

Bill didn't stop to question why, but there were no fluids coming from his wounds. No blood and no water: nothing. Then somehow, Bill was able to move a little bit. He dragged himself across the floor to the barred door. Then for some reason, the creatures allowed him to crawl out of the cell without stopping him.

When he exited the cell, his first instinct was to get as far away as possible. Bill was desperate. He wanted to get on his feet and run, but every move to get up took great effort.

But when he was able to stand, he could not run. He was seized with fear as he heard the horrified screams of an untold multitude of people crying out in torment. The sound was absolutely deafening. Then Bill entered a state of panic when he finally realized, *I'm in hell! This is a real place, and I'm actually here!*

Bill didn't understand. He thought, *Not me. I'm a good person.* The fear he was experiencing was so intense, he couldn't bear it; but again, he couldn't die. There was a whole world going on in the lower parts of the earth—a place so terrifying, so intense, and so hostile that it would be impossible for him to exaggerate the horror.

Bill looked to the right and could faintly see flames from afar that dimly lit the skyline. He realized that the flames were coming from a large pit, a gigantic raging inferno. The flames were intense, but the darkness seemed to swallow up the light. The skyline was barely invisible.

The only visible area he could see was that which the flames exposed. The ground was all rocky, barren, and desolate. There was not one living thing—it was a complete wasteland. There was not one green thing, not one blade of grass, and not a leaf on the ground.

Extreme thirst and dryness were one of the worst sensations Bill experienced. There was no water anywhere and no humidity in the air. He was desperate for just one drop of water.

He realized that this horror would last for an eternity; the thought of this thrust him back into a frantic state of mind. It didn't even enter his thoughts to call on God for help because he was there as one who didn't know God. The Lord didn't even come to mind.

He was then carried back into his cell by one of those demonic creatures. It threw him on the floor, and the other creature quickly grabbed his head and began to crush it. They treated him like he was lifeless prey. There are no words to describe how terrified Bill was.

But before they pulled his body apart, suddenly, he was taken out of the cell and placed next to that pit of fire he had viewed from a distance earlier. He felt comfort, knowing that he was snatched from the grip of those hideous creatures. But now he found himself next to an enormous pit with raging flames of fire leaping high into an open cavern. He could hear the pitiful screams of untold multitudes.

The heat was beyond unbearable. It was raining fire and burning rock, like the way lava falls from the sky when a volcano explodes. The smoke from the flames was very thick, allowing visibility for only a short distance. He was horrified when he saw people reaching out of the pit of fire, desperately trying to claw their way out. But there was no escape.

Suddenly, he began ascending through the tunnel. He didn't know how he was able to ascend or why. As he went up, he could view the vast wasteland of hell. He could now see more of the enormous pit, which looked to be as much as a mile across. However, this was just a fraction of hell's space. To the right of the large inferno were thousands of small pits, as far as he could see. Each pit was no more than three to five feet across and four to five feet deep—each pit holding a single lost soul.

As he continued to ascend upward, suddenly, a burst of light invaded the entire tunnel. It was a white light such as he had never seen before—so brilliant, so pure. It was so bright that he could not see the face of the one who was before him, but he instantly knew who he was.

Bill said, "Jesus," and he said, "I Am." Bill fell at His feet. It was as if he died. It seemed as if only a few moments had passed when he regained his awareness. He was still at His feet.

Words can't explain the range of emotions he experienced in the presence of the Lord. Just a moment before, he had been in the bowels of hell, just like someone who didn't know Jesus and was cursed and damned to eternal torment.

As soon as Jesus appeared, He restored an awareness to his mind that he was a Christian. Peace had replaced terror, and safety took the place of danger. The feelings of worthlessness, shame, and humiliation disappeared. At that moment, Bill was so grateful that he knew Jesus, that he was a Christian. He just wanted to worship Him.

Jesus reached down and touched his shoulder. His strength instantly returned, and he rose to his feet. Bill's next thought was, *why did you send me to this awful place?*

Before he could ask the question, Jesus answered, "Because many people do not believe that hell truly exists. Even some of my own people do not believe that hell is real."

As Bill stood there before the Lord, he thought, *why did You choose me for this experience?* There was no answer. To this day, he still doesn't know why the Lord decided to choose him for this experience.

Jesus continued, "Go and tell them about this place. It is not my desire that anyone should go there. Hell was made for the devil and his angels."

Bill replied, "Yes, of course I'll go."

It is God's will for all to be saved, and Bill had the most compelling desire to do His will. He felt so honored to do something that would please Him.

Then the thought crossed his mind, *why would anyone believe me?*

They will think that I had a bad dream or that I am crazy.

The Lord said to him, "It is not your job to convince their hearts. That responsibility belongs to the Holy Spirit. It is your part to go and tell them."

Bill was relieved to know that it was not his responsibility to convince anyone. The Lord gave him the easy part—all he had to do was open his mouth and tell the people, and He would draw them to Himself.

Jesus allowed him to see a steady stream of people falling through a tunnel—one after the other, after the other, after the other—into an open cavern, into the terror that he had just escaped. While he was watching this scene, Jesus allowed him to feel just a small amount of the sorrow He feels for His creation going to hell.

Bill said, "Please stop!" He couldn't bear it.

It was the deepest insight into God's feelings that he had during this whole experience. There's truly no way to measure how much He truly loves all people. When a single soul is lost to the devil and damned to that horrible place forever, it saddens Him greatly.

Bill asked Him, "Why didn't I know You when I was there?"

He said, "I kept it from you."

For Bill to experience the hopelessness of those souls in hell, the fact that he knew Jesus had to be hidden from his mind. If he knew Him there (as he has since 1970), he would have had hope that Jesus would rescue him. To experience the feeling of being lost forever was, by far, the worst part of hell.

Finally, Jesus said, "Tell them I am coming very, very soon."

Bill felt an urgency to warn as many people as possible, as time was running out.

He sternly said it again: "Tell them I am coming very, very soon!"

As Bill was having this time with Jesus, they kept ascending up the tunnel. They came to the earth's surface, and then they continued upward. They went high above the earth until they were out of the atmosphere.

Bill looked down and could see the curve of the earth. It was absolutely breathtaking. Bill could feel God's power, and he knew that everything was perfectly in His control.

Then they began moving back toward the earth. They reentered the atmosphere and quickly made their way toward Bill's home. As they hovered over his house, Bill could see through the roof. As he looked into the living room, he was startled to see his body lying on the living room floor. Bill then passed through the roof and into his living room. As he approached his body, he seemed to be drawn back into it. It was at that time that the Lord left.

When the Lord left, immediately, the horrors of hell came back into his mind. Bill started screaming and lay there in a traumatized state. His cries were loud enough to reach the bedroom and wake his wife from a deep sleep.

His wife, Annette, got out of bed and walked down the hallway to the living room, where she found Bill in a fetal position with his hands grasping at the sides of his head. His breathing was erratic, and he was screaming, "I feel like I'm going to die! The Lord took me to hell. Pray for me! Pray that the Lord will take the fear from my mind!"

She had never seen him this way. He is a reserved, calm person. Those that know him would tell you he is very even-tempered, steady, and consistent, and has been so all his life. For Bill to be out of control and traumatized like that was completely against his nature.

After a short while, Bill began to calm down and regain his composure. His screaming subsided, his breathing returned to normal, and he was able to gather his thoughts. He then asked his wife for a glass of water.

Bill was amazed as he looked at the water in the glass that Annette handed him. It was life in a glass. He gulped it down and asked for another. Bill never wanted to be thirsty again.

Bill Wiese is now spending the rest of his life telling the story of what he saw, heard, and felt in that place of torment.

Chapter Fourteen

The Place Called Heaven

ONE DAY BEFORE Jesus went to the cross, He gave a promise to every person who would choose to receive Him as his or her Lord and Savior. He said,

> Let not your heart be troubled: You believe in God, believe also in Me. In my Father's house are many mansions: if it were not so, I would have told you. I go to prepare a place for you. And if I go and prepare a place for you, I will come again, and receive you unto myself; that where I am, there you may be also.
>
> John 14:1–3

The Bible teaches us that there are three heavens: The atmosphere above the earth is the first heaven. The starry space is the second heaven. This second heaven that consists of the starry space is huge. When you go out on a clear, moonless night, all the stars in the sky number to perhaps five thousand stars at any given time.

Our sun is a star. It's just the one that is closest to us. It has been estimated that one million earths could fit inside the sun. That's how huge our sun is, and yet some of those stars that we see on a starry night are bigger than our sun.

To give you an idea of how huge the second heaven is, the family of stars in which our sun and moon belongs to is called the Milky Way galaxy. It has been estimated that there are perhaps one hundred billion galaxies in the second heaven.

And then there is the heaven of heavens, which the Bible calls "the third heaven" (2 Corinthians 12:2). The heaven of heavens that sits on top of the universe is where God's throne is. This is where God lives, and God lives in an awesome place.

1979 Visit to Heaven

In October 1979, a pastor came home from a meeting and found his wife crouched down on their staircase, weeping uncontrollably. He knew immediately that something was seriously wrong.

He soon learned that his ten-year-old son brought a small television set into the bathroom to watch a football game while taking a bath. He accidentally pulled the TV into the bathtub and was electrocuted.

He had no pulse, and his flesh was cold and blue; his eyes were fully dilated, which indicated no brain activity. The paramedics arrived, and for forty-five minutes, they tried to revive him but were unsuccessful. They were now becoming restless and were getting ready to give up.

Then the boy's father prayed, "Father, I don't have any more faith. I've exhausted mine, but I know that in Your Word, you speak of another faith." (He was referring to what the Bible calls the gift of faith.)

Suddenly, the father felt something like a hand on the top of his head. Then he sensed a very strong force and authority rising from within his spirit, and he shouted at his son, "You will live and not die in the name of Jesus!"

All of a sudden, the EKG machine started beeping, with pulse motions appearing on the screen. The paramedics jumped with excitement. By the time they got him down the stairs, he went from blue to pink; his eyes were fully restored, and his body was now warm.

Three days after he was out of the hospital, the father saw that his son's face was glowing. He asked, "What's going on?"

His son replied, "Dad, I've been with Jesus. When the TV hit the bathtub, I didn't feel a thing. A huge angel grabbed my right arm and took me right out of my body. We flew through a tunnel at an amazing rate of acceleration. We hit the speed of light before landing on one of the streets of heaven." He explained that the streets were not golden but made of pure gold; he could see through them. (Gold in its purest state is transparent.)

The boy shared that the first people to greet him on the street were relatives who had died, and he named each of them, some of whom he had never met or even knew by name; however, his mom and dad knew them. There was also in this welcoming group a lady named

Phyllis. She was a neighbor whom the boy's mother had prayed for to receive Jesus a month before he was electrocuted. She had died two weeks after her conversion.

They were all conversing when, suddenly, he heard rustling, and the group around him split apart. There stood Jesus. The Lord took the boy on a tour of heaven.

There were many streets and buildings; it was a large city. The flowers, grass, and even rocks were all alive and singing in harmony. He said that it was as if they were praising God. If he stepped on grass or on a flower, it wouldn't be crushed but immediately rebounded to its previous position. He noticed that the colors were vibrant and bright, much more so than he'd seen on earth. There were even colors he'd never seen before. He also got the privilege of seeing his mother, father, and two siblings' mansions.

Then came the shock; Jesus told the boy that he had to go back. He didn't want to leave heaven, but then Jesus brought him to a place where He pulled open a veil where he could see his father calling him back. Jesus then said, "He is your father and has the authority to call you back."

Since that time, the boy has told his father to never call him back if he happens to die again.

Roberts Liardon

When Roberts Liardon was a young Christian, he matured spiritually far beyond his years. He was a student at Victory Christian School, and he was respected by students, teachers, and administrators. Roberts provided a consistent model of Christian character.

Probably one of the reasons Roberts matured spiritually beyond his years and is a consistent model of Christian character is because of the two encounters he had with Jesus when he was a child.

He had a heavenly experience with Jesus when he was eight years old and an earthly experience with Jesus when he was eleven years old.

This earthly experience he had with Jesus when he was eleven was when he was at home, watching the old sitcom, the *Laverne and Shirley* show. While he was watching the show, all of a sudden, Jesus walked in through the front door and came over and sat down on the couch next to him, and He sort of glanced at the TV, and it shut off. Everything shut off, and all that Roberts heard was Jesus, and all he saw was His glory.

Jesus said to him, "Roberts, I want you to study the lives of my generals in my great army throughout time."

Now who are these generals that Jesus was talking about? The Bible teaches us that when a person receives Jesus Christ as their Lord and Savior, he or she enters God's army, and he or she becomes a soldier of the Lord. The war that we fight is not against other people; it's against Satan and his demon spirits who not only come against us personally but who also are scattered throughout the atmosphere of this earth to wreak havoc upon mankind and who use people to work through to steal, kill, and destroy other people's lives.

As soldiers of the Lord Jesus Christ in God's army, God has given us generals to help train us. The Bible teaches us that when Jesus arose from the dead, He gave us apostles, prophets, evangelists, pastors, and teachers.

God anoints these generals with the power of the Holy Spirit and works through them to train God's people—to perfect them, to train them to minister to others, to build them up, and to teach them how to fight the good fight of faith and be victorious in this life's journey.

Therefore it is important to go to church. You go there in order to receive training, and that will help prepare you to live a victorious life. Obviously, there are things that you receive from these individuals that you cannot get in your own private time of prayer and study.

If you are going to a church where they are not training you to live a victorious Christian life, get out of that church and ask God where He wants you to go.

So, Jesus appears to Roberts and says, "Roberts, I want you to study the lives of my generals in my great army throughout time. Know them like the back of your hand. Know why they were a success. Know why they failed, and you will lack nothing in that area. Roberts, if you will be faithful in this thing, I will promote you." Then Jesus got up, walked back out the door, and the TV clicked back on.

After that day, Roberts said that he had to leave the TV alone. He turned his back on school and sports; he left everything, including his best friend, to do what God called him to do.

Then one day, I remember walking into a bookstore and seeing several of the largest books I had ever seen. They were books written about God's generals in times past, written by Roberts. He was obedient to doing what Jesus told him to do.

But this is the second experience that Roberts had with Jesus. The first experience took place when Roberts was only eight years old. Roberts's grandmother and grandfather were pastors, and during their ministry, they started over twenty churches. Later, his grandfather died, and his grandmother came to live with Roberts and his family.

After his grandmother moved in, Roberts remembered all the prayer that took place in his home. He said that there was more prayer in his home than there was in church. He also saw more of the power of God, more healings, more evidence of God in his home than he did in church.

Roberts knew from this young age that God had called him to preach. Therefore, his grandmother spent much of her time training Roberts for the ministry. Her "training" mostly involved prayer and reading the Bible.

In the summer of 1974, when Roberts was eight years old, he went into his room after school to read the Bible. His assignment for the day was to read four chapters of the Gospel of John, and he was in a hurry because he wanted to go out and play with his friends. So, he grabbed his Bible and was getting ready to read the first chapter when suddenly, his Bible, his room, and even his body disappeared!

He had no warning. Suddenly, the real Roberts, who is a spirit being, was soaring through the heavens at a high rate of speed. He saw many things as he zoomed through the heavens and then finally landed outside the biggest gate he had ever seen or has ever seen since. It was very wide, very tall and had no cut or blemish on it. This gate was made of one solid pearl—one immense, glossy, glowing white pearl—and the edges were carved with a design.

Then he heard the voice of a man that said, "This is one of the gates."

Roberts turned around, and there stood Jesus in all His glory! Immediately, he recognized Him, although He did not look like any of the pictures he had seen. But somehow, he knew who He was.

The most outstanding impression Roberts had of Jesus when looking at Him was that He was a perfect man. The way He looked, talked, and moved was perfect.

Roberts buckled to his knees, and tears began to stream down his face. He couldn't stop crying.

Then Jesus spoke again and said, "I want to give you a tour through heaven because I love you so much. Now no more tears. But a face full of joy would make me glad." Then Jesus laughed, and then Roberts laughed, and Jesus came over and picked Roberts up and dried away his tears. Jesus then escorted Roberts through that huge gate, and He didn't ask anybody to open it, and He didn't push a button. It just opened by itself.

The first thing Roberts saw was a street, and it was gold. Later, when he walked through heaven, he saw that all the streets were literally made of pure gold. And the curbs were lined with flowers in all colors of the rainbow.

When Roberts first saw this street made of gold, he thought, *if this is heaven, then these are gold streets I'm standing on.* Roberts took off running toward the curb, and from a distance, he saw that Jesus turned to say something to him, but Roberts had taken off.

Jesus said, "What are you doing over there?"

Roberts was standing on the grass alongside the curb, with his eyes and mouth wide open in surprise, and he answered Jesus with two words: "Golden streets!"

Roberts said that Jesus laughed and laughed. He thought He was never going to stop. Then He said, "Come over here."

Roberts said, "No. Those streets are gold. I can't walk on them!" The only time Roberts had seen gold was in rings on people's fingers, and he knew it was very expensive and very valuable.

Jesus said, "Come on." Jesus kept laughing as He walked over to where Roberts was and led him back on the street. Jesus said, "These streets were made for those who have accepted Me into their hearts, so enjoy them."

Roberts said that the atmosphere in heaven is wonderful; the very breezes were filled with the presence of God. There is a feeling of inner warmth of being wrapped in a blanket of God's love.

They passed towns, buildings, and little offices. The buildings were for whatever "business" or interaction that takes place in heaven. He saw people coming and going, and they were all smiling. Some of them sang songs that he recognized on earth, and some of them sang heavenly songs that he had never heard before.

He noticed that they carried little bundles, and some of them carried little books. It appeared that people were going in and out of those buildings to get things. He saw one woman walk into a building with a bundle in her hand and walked out of the building with a book.

Then they walked on through a certain section in heaven that was really like a small town, and he saw street signs. They came to one of the street signs, and he doesn't remember the name of it, but he remembers them turning right on the street. Then they walked on what looked like an unpaved dirt path, and he saw a gigantic house above the streets.

He said that Jesus talked to him the whole time they walked up this dirt pathway. Jesus is not only our Savior, but He also wants to be a friend to us. He desires a relationship with us.

When they got to the door of this mansion, Jesus walked up and knocked on the door. He didn't just walk in. One aspect of love is being considerate of other people's feelings, time, and privacy. They waited about three minutes and then knocked again.

Then a little gentleman opened the door, stuck his head out, and spoke to them. He said, "How are you doing, Jesus? And how are you doing, Roberts?"

He was surprised that this man knew his name. But he remembered that it seemed like everybody knew his name in heaven. At least, those they met.

The man invited them in, and Roberts sat down on a black velvet couch. He found that the heavenly furniture was somewhat different to earthly furniture. Earthly furniture sometimes becomes somewhat uncomfortable. Sometimes you must move around, trying to get comfortable. But when he sat on this couch, comfort reached up and cuddled him. He was so comfortable he didn't have to move once. In heaven, comfort finds you.

After they finished talking, the man took them through the house, and his mansion seemed just like the houses on earth, but it was total perfection.

Another experience Roberts had with Jesus was when they came to a branch of the river of life. He assumed that there was only one river in heaven, although there may be more, he only saw one. The Bible describes this river as being crystal bright, flowing from the throne of God (Rev. 22:1).

When they walked up to the river of life, they didn't just look at it but walked into it. It was knee-deep and perfectly clear. Unlike a river on earth, it doesn't just flow around you. It flows through you, and you feel a surge of energy coming out of that water and into your being.

Then Jesus did something that is quite personal and extremely precious to Roberts. The Lord Jesus, the Holy Son of God, reached over and dunked him in the water of the river of life.

So, Roberts got back up, splashed Jesus, and they proceeded right there to have a water fight, splashing each other and laughing.

This experience for Roberts meant something profound to him. Jesus, the King of glory, took time out for little eight-year-old Roberts to play with him in the river of life.

When they eventually got out of the water, it was as if a giant hair dryer then began to blow and dry their clothes instantly.

Roberts saw many other things and had other various experiences in heaven such as when they were walking along, and Jesus began to cry. Roberts said that he was astounded. Jesus Christ, the Son of God, began to cry.

Jesus turned toward Roberts while He was crying, and there were things He said that were too sacred to repeat, but this one thing He told him he could tell.

Jesus said, "Roberts, I love my people so much that I would go back to earth, preach my three years over again, and die for just one person. If I had not already paid the price for them, and if I thought they wanted to come to heaven, I would do it all over again.

"I would not have to know they would make it. If I just thought they wanted to come, I would do it for them, even if they were the greatest sinners of all.

"I love my people so much. Why do people not take Me at my word? Do they not know that I have all power in heaven and on earth to back up what I said? It is so easy. I made it so simple. If people would just take Me at my word, I will do what I said."

God made an investment in this young boy, Roberts Liardon. God has blessed Roberts with a gift of unusually strong preaching. He has answered a worldwide calling of

God. He has preached in ninety-four nations and was twice elected as the most outstanding young man in America.

Roberts is a best-selling author who has written over forty books, some of which have been translated in over forty-seven languages, and his audiotapes and videotapes have helped to strengthen and change people all over the world.

Chapter Fifteen

Choose Your Destiny

THIS DAY HAS brought every one of us one day closer to experiencing something we have never experienced before, breathing our last breath, separating from our body and going out into eternity.

When that day comes, do you know yet if you are going to heaven or hell?

This life's journey is a test for mankind to see who is going to heaven and who is going to hell when they die.

The Bible tells us that it is appointed unto mankind once to die, but after this is the judgment.

So, the bottom line is, there are two sides to life—the winning side and the losing side. The winning side is God's side, and everyone who is not on God's side will lose.

Judgment day is coming, and you need to make sure that you are not going to receive a guilty verdict because if you do, that will mean eternal damnation for you for all of eternity.

Every one of us is born into this world separated from a relationship with God. Those who receive Jesus Christ as their Lord and Savior become reconciled to God and enter a relationship with him.

All those who are presently in hell today will eventually be taken from that place of torment to stand before God on Judgment Day.

> *Then I saw a great white throne and Him who sat on it, from whose face the earth and the heaven fled away. And there was found no place for them. And I saw the dead, small and great, standing before God, and books were opened. And another book was opened, which is the Book of Life. And the dead were judged according to their works, by the things which were written in the books.*
>
> *The sea gave up the dead who were in it, and Death and Hades delivered up*

the dead which were in them. And they were judged, each one according to their works. Then Death and Hades were cast into the lake of fire. This is the second death. And anyone not found written in the Book of Life was cast into the lake of fire.

Revelation 20:11–15

All those who are presently in torment today will eventually be cast into the lake of fire. People are sent from this life into the place of torment because they have not accepted Jesus Christ and because their names are not written in the book of life.

A man is not sent to hell because of the sins he has committed. He is sent because he is an unbeliever—because he has never accepted Jesus Christ as his Lord and Savior.

The message of the cross and God's command to repent is for mankind in every part of the earth. God commands men everywhere to repent regardless of their background, social status, educational degrees, or skin color. There is no other option and no way out of this divine command. It is God's requirement for every person on earth if he or she intends to enter the kingdom of heaven.

If you don't know Jesus as your personal Lord and Savior, I would like to take this opportunity to introduce you to the greatest friend you'll ever have. As you say these words, if you'll believe them with your heart, you'll be born again:

> *"Jesus, come into my life. Forgive me for all my sins. I ask you to cleanse me and make me a new person in You right now. I believe that You are the Son of God and that You died on the cross for me. Jesus, I want to thank You for loving me enough to die for me. I accept all that Your shed blood bought for me on the cross, and I receive You as my Savior and Lord. In Your name, I pray. Amen."*

Evidence, Facts, And Proof

AS I SAID previously in this book, my parents became Christians when I was a child. I was brought up in church and was taught that God is real, and that the Bible is true and that there is a heaven and a hell. I simply took their word for it.

I did not take God very seriously during my upbringing. But in my teenage years, I became concerned about my eternity and eventually made the decision to cross over onto God's side of the line.

Not too long after I crossed over, I began the process of praying, reading the Bible, going to church—I was practicing doing what the Bible says to do. It was during this process when I began finding out by experience that God is real, and that the Bible is true. I began to experience what the Bible says that I would experience.

I am an individual who stands in a position of strength because I know by experience. A man with an argument is no match for a man with experience.

Millions and millions of Christians around the world are experiencing the same thing. When you read the Bible or hear it being taught or preached and when you practice doing what it says to do, you experience what God says you will experience, and you receive what God says you will receive.

It was God himself who taught us in the Bible that it's not those who merely read the Bible or hear it being taught or preached who experience what God says you will experience, but it's those who do what it says who receives the blessing.

A Word to the Atheist

Now let me speak to those of you who don't even believe in God. It doesn't matter whether you believe in God or not. He is still real.

Let me ask you a question: When you look at a building, how do you know there was a builder? What evidence do you have that tells you that somebody built that building?

The building is proof that there was a builder.

When you look at a painting, how do you know there was a painter? What evidence do you have that tells you that somebody painted that painting?

The painting is proof that somebody painted that painting.

When you look at the creation—the sun, moon, and stars, and when you look at our physical bodies and the way they were designed and intricately made, how do you know there was a Creator? What evidence do you have that tells you that somebody created or brought creation into existence?

Creation is proof that there is a creator.

Antony Flew

One of the world's most prominent atheists was a man by the name of Antony Flew. For fifty years, he taught at Oxford, Aberdeen, and other world-class universities and wrote more than a dozen books attacking the existence of God.

But then something major happened. Newspapers around the planet began reporting that Antony Flew changed his mind. He publicly declared that he had been wrong. He said that he now believes in a supernatural creator.

When he was asked what evidence caused such a massive shift to his belief in God, he explained, "Einstein felt that there must be intelligence behind the integrated complexity of the physical world. If this is a sound argument, the integrated complexity of the organic world is just inordinately greater—all creatures are complicated pieces of design. So, an argument that is important about the physical world is immeasurably stronger when applied to the biological world."

The scientific discoveries over the last fifty years conclude that God exists, and that's why Flew, and many other atheists have changed their mind.

Antony Flew said, "I had to go wherever the evidence took me."

If you want all the details as to how the world's most prominent atheist changed his mind, check out Antony Flews' last book, *There Is a God.*

Modern Science

Even modern science points to the fact that we must really matter to God! The more physicists, biologists, and other scientists learn about the universe, the better we understand how it is uniquely suited for our existence, custom-made with the exact specifications that make human life possible. The universe was designed by God to support and nourish human life.

Raise or lower the universe's rate of expansion by even one part in a million, and it would have ruled out the possibility of human life.

If the average distance between stars were any greater, planets, like the earth, would not have been formed; if it was any smaller, the planetary orbits necessary for life would not have occurred.

If the ratio of carbon to oxygen had been slightly different than it is, none of us would have been here to breathe the air.

Change the tilt of the earth's axis slightly to one direction, and we would freeze. Change it to the other direction, and we would burn up.

Suppose that the earth had been a bit closer or farther from the sun or just a little smaller or that it rotated at a speed any different from the one we're spinning at right now. Given any of these changes, the resulting temperature variations would have been completely fatal.

Lee Strobel

It has been said that science is the search for truth. Many people in the twentieth century chose to be atheists because they simply didn't have enough evidence at that time that would prove there was any such thing as God. One of those individuals was a man by the name of Lee Strobel.

During his academic years, he was convinced by science that there was no such thing as God. In Strobel's mind, the very idea of a creator was irrelevant. Science didn't teach it; therefore, he didn't believe in God.

Then later in his life, his wife, Leslie, made a startling announcement to him. She said, "I have decided to become a follower of Jesus."

His natural reaction of his wife's conversion to Christianity was to get angry. He asked his wife impolitely, "What has gotten into you?" He couldn't understand how a rational person as his wife could buy into an irrational religious concoction of wishful thinking, make-believe, mythology, and legend.

In the following months, he often expressed his anger by slamming doors, belittling his wife's newfound faith, lashing out against her church, and gradually increasing his use and abuse of alcohol. One day, in his frustration, he even kicked a hole into their living room wall.

But also, in the following months, he watched how his wife's character began to change. Her values underwent a transformation. She became a more loving and caring and authentic person. Her life was being changed for the better.

He also saw this major change take place in another person's life. Lee Strobel, who was a reporter for the *Chicago Tribune*, did a story concerning a man by the name of Ron Bronski.

Ron Bronski had been in and out of the court system ever since he threw a hammer at someone's head when he was eight years old. He was second in command of a vicious street gang called Belairs that ruled parts of Chicago. He had his occasional run-ins with the law, but then he got himself into big-time trouble when he was twenty-one. Ron made a vow of revenge when a member of a street gang brutally assaulted one of his friends.

He found the guy's brother; whose name was Gary. Ron then shoved a gun into Gary's chest and pulled the trigger. But the gun misfired. Ron pointed the gun in the air and pulled the trigger, and this time, it went off. Gary took off running, and Ron ran after him, shooting as he ran. One of the bullets tore into Gary's back and lodged itself next to his liver, and he fell forward on the pavement.

After he flipped him over, Gary started pleading for his life. "Don't shoot me, man! Don't shoot me again! Don't kill me!"

Ron had no compassion, and without hesitation, he shoved the gun in Gary's face and pulled the trigger again. But this time, the gun was empty.

Suddenly, a siren went off, and Ron managed to escape the police. A warrant was issued out for Ron's arrest on a charge of attempted murder. Adding this to his previous police record, that would mean twenty years in prison.

Ron decided to avoid prosecution and took off with his girlfriend to Chicago and finally ended up in Portland, Oregon, where Ron got his first real job, working in a metal shop.

The people he was working with happened to be Christians. Ron became impressed with these people, and through their influence and the work of the Holy Spirit, Ron became a radically committed follower of Jesus.

As time passed, Ron's character and values began to change. He married his girlfriend, who also became a Christian. Ron was a good worker, participated in church activities, and was a well-respected member of the community. The police stopped looking for him long ago, and he was safe to live out the rest of his days in Portland.

But there was a problem. His conscience bothered him. Even though he got things right with God, he didn't get it right with society. He realized that he was living a lie, which he couldn't tolerate now that he was a Christian. So, after giving this situation much prayer, he decided to get on a train, head to Chicago, and face the charges against him.

When Ron appeared in court, he didn't come in like many others who offered excuses for their bad behavior. He looked at the judge and said, "I'm guilty. I did it. I'm responsible. If I need to go to prison, that's okay. But I've become a Christian, and the right thing to do is to admit what I have done and to ask for forgiveness. What I did was wrong—plain and simple. And I'm sorry. I really am."

Lee Strobel was so impressed that he asked Ron about his faith. Ron shared with Lee his entire story, and what he told him was so amazing that Lee needed to investigate the facts. He questioned his coworkers, friends, and pastor in Oregon, as well as the street-toughened detectives who knew him in Chicago.

Every one of them was in agreement that something had dramatically transformed him. Ron claimed that God was the one who was responsible.

Ron expected to spend twenty years behind bars away from his wife and little girl. But the judge was so deeply impressed with Ron's changed life that he concluded that he wasn't a threat to society anymore and gave him probation instead. The judge said, "Go home and be with your family."

Lee Strobel was blown away. He had never seen anything like this before. After the court was adjourned, he rushed into the hallway to interview Ron. Lee asked Ron, "What's your reaction to what the judge just did?"

Ron looked deep into the eyes of Lee Strobel and said, "What that judge did was show me grace—sort of like what Jesus did. And, Lee, can I tell you something? If you let Him, God will show you grace too. Don't forget that."

Searching for Answers

Lee's interest and attention was aroused. He was amazed at the changes that took place in his wife, Leslie, and was blown away by the testimony of Ron Bronski. They received Jesus Christ as their Lord and Savior, and their lives were being changed for the better.

So, he decided to investigate what was going on, and Lee was very good at investigating. He was an award-winning legal editor of the *Chicago Tribune*. He was a journalist for fourteen years at the *Chicago Tribune* and other newspapers, winning top honors in Illinois for investigative reporting. He was determined to go wherever the answers would take him. His multifaceted spiritual investigation lasted nearly two years.

Lee said that the one thing that was difficult for him was getting beyond his prejudices. For many years, he had a lot of motivation to stay on the atheistic path. He didn't want there to be a God who would hold him responsible for his immoral lifestyle.

But the evidence was too overwhelming for Lee. The scientific discoveries over the past few decades clearly point toward God—an intelligent designer of mankind and the universe. As a result, many people, including scientists, are now turning their hearts and minds toward God.

Lee Strobel knows that there are many people who are just like he was, who believe that Christianity is nothing but an irrational religious concoction of wishful thinking, make-believe, mythology, and legend.

Therefore, he did something about it. He became a *New York Times* best-selling author of more than two dozen books, giving the people of this world all the evidence, facts, and proof that God is real and that the Bible is true.

The Unfair Advantage

When it comes to Christianity versus atheism, it would seem that Christians have an unfair advantage. The national spokesman for American atheists said:

> You Christians are alike. You give the case for Christ, but you don't tell the other side of the story. Wouldn't it be great if we could lay out the case for atheism, and you could lay out the case for Christianity, and we could just let the audience decide for themselves?

Then Lee Strobel—who, as I stated earlier, was a former atheist but was now a best-selling author of Christianity—responded,

> Let's do just that. You go out and find the strongest defender of atheism you can—your best and brightest. Our church will bring him here from any-

where in the world, and we'll go out and get a top-notch proponent of Christianity.

So, the atheists chose Frank Zindler, who was a top debater for an atheistic organization, to represent the atheist side. Zindler was a former professor of geology and biology. He was a person who vigorously promoted atheism in articles and books and on television and radio programs.

William Lane Craig was the one who was to present the Christian case. Craig had doctorates in philosophy and theology. He was an author, professor, and one of the top defenders of Christianity in the world.

The debate topic that they agreed upon was "Atheism versus Christianity: Where Does the Evidence Point?"

The *Chicago Tribune* wrote four articles on the event. A total of 117 radio stations would broadcast the debate live.

On the night of the debate, traffic became gridlocked around the church from people flocking to the event. They opened the doors of the church one full hour before the start time, and people ran down the aisles to get a seat. About 7,778 people showed up, filling the main auditorium and several other rooms linked by video. The atmosphere was electric.

When the curtains went up, Craig began spelling out five powerful arguments for God and Christianity. Then Zindler gave forth what he thought was evidence for atheism.

They went back and forth for two hours, and at the end of the debate, members of the audience were asked to set aside their personal beliefs and vote for whichever side had presented the strongest case.

When the results came in, 97 percent declared that the Christian case prevailed. Even the people who were not Christians, an overwhelming 82 percent concluded that the evidence offered for Christianity was the most compelling.

Unbelievers who listened to both sides walked out as believers, and not a single person became an atheist.

A Word to the Skeptic

God is real, and the Bible is true. All you must do is examine the evidence, facts, and proof and go where the evidence takes you.

When someone is on trial, they look for facts that can be proven beyond a reasonable doubt. These facts are established through information regarding what an eyewitness saw; sounds a reliable witness heard; incriminating evidence such as fingerprints, footprints, hair, or blood found in the area; and written documents and receipts, bank records, surveillance videos and so forth.

Then through these evidence and facts that prove beyond a reasonable doubt, they are then able to draw conclusions that allow them to throw people into prison for life or sometimes even put them to death.

Why not put the Bible to the test? The Bible is unique. Of all the printed materials in the world, the Bible is the number one best-seller. It is different from all others. It stands in a category all by itself, and no other book compares to it. It has been read by more people and published in more languages than any other book in history. It is the most important book ever because it reveals the will of God for His creation.

The Bible has withstood the test of time, the test of history, the test of archaeology, the test of science, and the test of prophetic fulfillment. Prophecy is where God predicts the future. It's where God says, "This is going to happen in the future. Watch and see that what I say will come to pass." And then it happens, just like God says it would happen.

Repeatedly, what God said would happen in the future has happened and is happening just like God says it would happen. It has been estimated that one-third of the entire Bible is prophecy, and not one prophecy of the entire Bible has ever failed to come to pass.

Josh McDowell

There are many people who absolutely will not believe the gospel of Jesus Christ unless they have evidence and facts that prove the Bible to be true. A man by the name of Josh McDowell was this kind of person.

As a young teenager, Josh wanted to be happy. He wanted to be one of the happiest individuals in the entire world. But he also wanted meaning in life. He wanted answers to questions like "Who am I?" "Why in the world am I here?" "Where am I going?"

So, Josh began searching for answers, and he was always very practical. If something didn't work, he just chucked it. Josh went, year after year, trying to find the purpose for life and didn't find it yet.

Later, when he was in college, he became the freshman class president and was very popular with the students. Josh threw more parties with the students' money than anybody else did. But Josh didn't let the students know how unhappy he was. In fact, those around him thought that he was one of the most happy-go-lucky guys around. During their political campaigns, they used the phrase "happiness is Josh."

But what they didn't realize was that Josh would wake up on Monday morning usually with a headache from the night before, and his attitude was "Well, here goes another five days." Happiness for Josh revolved around three nights of the week—Friday night, Saturday night, and Sunday night—and then the vicious cycle would begin all over again.

Josh's happiness was like so many other people's happiness. It was only skin-deep. It depended on his circumstances. If things were going well, Josh was happy. If things were not going well, he wasn't happy. Josh was very sincere in trying to find meaning, truth, and purpose to life, but he hadn't found it yet.

But in and around the university, something started catching Josh's eye. There was a small group of people—eight students and two faculty members—who had something different about their lives. These people seemed to know where they were going, and that was unusual among university students. These people didn't just talk about love. They got involved. They seemed to be rising above the circumstances of university life while it seemed that everybody else was under a pile.

One important thing he noticed about these people was that they had a joyful characteristic that was not dependent on their circumstances. They were disgustingly happy. They had something that Josh didn't have, so Josh decided to make friends with these people.

Two weeks after his decision, Josh was sitting around the table while most of the group members were present, and they were making conversation. Then the subject started getting around to God, and Josh started getting uncomfortable. The reason Josh was getting uncomfortable was because previously, he had a problem with Christians.

Christians bothered Josh. Josh thought that all Christians were ugly. He thought that most Christians were walking idiots. He would wait for a Christian to speak up in the classroom so he could tear him or her up one side and down the other. Josh imagined that if a Christian had a single brain cell, it would die of loneliness.

So, Josh was sitting around this group of people he was interested in, and the subject started getting around to God. Josh started getting uncomfortable, so he leaned back in his chair because he didn't want anybody to think he had any desire for what they were talking about.

Eventually, Josh leaned over to one of the girls in this group, and he said, "Tell me, what changed your lives? Why are your lives so different from the other students and from the leaders on campus and from the professors? Why?"

This young lady looked straight into Josh McDowell's eyes and said two words that Josh thought he would never hear as part of a solution in a university. She said, "Jesus Christ."

Josh said, "Oh, for god's sake, don't give me that garbage. I'm fed up with the church. I'm fed up with the Bible. Don't give me that garbage about religion!"

This woman must have had a lot of conviction because she shot right back, "Mister, I didn't say 'religion.' I said 'Jesus Christ'!"

She said something that Josh didn't know before. Christianity is not a religion. Religion is men and women trying to work their way to God through their good works. Christianity, on the other hand, is God coming to men and women through Jesus Christ, offering them a relationship with Himself.

Josh's new friends challenged him to examine the claims that Jesus Christ is God's Son, that He lived among real men and women, died on the cross for the sins of mankind, was raised from the dead, and could change a person's life in the twentieth century.

They challenged him repeatedly until he finally took their challenge. But he took their challenge to prove them wrong. In fact, the background of Josh's first two books was his setting out to prove that Christianity was wrong. But during his study, he found out that he was the one that was wrong. He didn't know there were facts that a person could examine. His mind finally concluded that Jesus Christ must have been who He claimed to be. Josh then chose to receive Jesus Christ as his Lord and Savior, and his life was changed.

Josh McDowell was once a skeptic who believed that most Christians are walking idiots and that if a Christian had a single brain cell, it would die of loneliness. He realized that there were many people who were just like him who had these kinds of feelings concerning Christians and Christianity, so he did something about it. He began reaching the spiritually skeptical and has been doing so for over five decades.

He has delivered more than twenty-four thousand talks to over fifteen million young people in 118 countries. He is the author or coauthor of 120 books. He has been writing book after book, providing the people of this world all the evidence, facts, and proof that God is real, that Jesus is who He claimed to be, and that the Bible is true.

Perfect Forgiveness

MANY PEOPLE BELIEVE that they have committed too many major sins for God to forgive them. They even say things like, "There's no way I would go into a church. The walls of the building would cave in." But I have good news for them: God's forgiveness is much more powerful than their sin. In fact, God's forgiveness is perfect!

No matter who you are or what you have done, you are the one Jesus died for. He came to save you—to rescue you. The Bible tells us that the angels of God throw a celebration every time a person gets saved. Angels live in the breathtaking presence of Almighty God and regularly see His wonders, which are beyond our imagination. Yet the angels are so thrilled about one soul who repents that they rejoice with great joy.

As I said previously in this book, the most tragic thing that took place when Satan became the god of this world system was when Satan's sin nature became lodged within the spirit of mankind. How does an individual become a sinner? Simply by being born into this world.

The sin nature lodged in our spirit caused us to be in bondage. It caused us to sin by habit. The Bible tells us that we became servants of sin (Romans 6:17).

The word *servant* comes from a word that was used in Ancient Greece as one of the most wretched expressions for a slave. It described a servant who was so totally sold into slavery that he had no destiny of his own. He was a slave to the desires of his owner.

This describes our slavery to sin before Jesus came into our lives. We may have thought we were in charge of our lives; we may have assumed that we were calling the shots ourselves. In reality, we were in the grip of sin, and our sin nature was controlling our lives and destinies. We were slaves to sin, captives sold into the depravity of slavery.

Then God Almighty came to our rescue. It was the will of the Father for Jesus to give His life for us. Jesus came into this world in order to buy us back from Satan's slave market. The Bible tells us that Jesus "gave Himself for us, that He might redeem us from all iniquity, and purify unto Himself a peculiar people, zealous of good works" (Titus 2:14).

The word redeem is one of the most important words in the New Testament. It comes from a Greek word that describes a person who paid a very high price to obtain the slave of his choice. Once the price was offered and accepted, that slave became his personal property.

When every one of us was born into this world, we were born into Satan's slave market. Jesus came into this world, into Satan's slave market because He was looking for us. He was not looking for a particular person; He was looking for all of us.

"While we were yet sinners, Christ died for us" (Romans 5:8). While we were living our lives in the total opposite of the way God wanted us to live, Jesus still paid the price for our sins on the cross.

> For God so loved the people of this
> world, that He gave His only begot-
> ten Son, that whoever believes [trusts

in, clings to, relies on] Him shall not
perish, but have eternal life.

John 3:16

In order to understand the love that God has for mankind, we need to look at the definition of the God kind of love. When the Bible talks about the love that God has for us, the word *love* comes from the Greek word *agape*, which means "to place a high value on an object."

Very early in Greek, the word *agape* was used to describe the admiration that a man had for an art object. The art object was so beautiful that it drew affection out of the onlooker's heart. He couldn't just look at it; he was affected when he looked at it. Admiration came out of his heart. Appreciation came out of his heart. He didn't have the words to express all that he felt because of the beauty of this object.

This tells us that when God looks at us, it draws something out of the heart of God. It's not a shallow love; it's a deep love. It's something that comes deep from within the heart of God when He sees His creation.

When God saw the people of this world who were separated from Him because of sin, something sprang out of the heart of God, and because of what He felt in

His heart, He was willing to give the sacrifice of His Son for it.

Before the foundation of this world, God had an awesome plan for every person who would be born into this world. Every one of us was created by God with a purpose in mind.

But then there came the fall of man. We were all born into this world, into Satan's slave market, which became a small interruption in God's eternal plan. The good news is that God is not looking at us for what we are; He is looking at the original plan He has for our lives. He is looking at what He, by His divine, miracle-working power, can make of us.

Therefore, Jesus came into Satan's slave market looking for every one of us. We are so precious to Him that He paid the highest price ever paid for a slave. The price was His very own blood! He purchased us out of Satan's slave market. He purchased us for Himself. He paid the ransom price, liberated us, and set us free from the bondage of sin.

Here are some examples of God's perfect forgiveness in action:

Skeeter and the Mafia

Marge Caldwell's church presented a Christian crusade at a football stadium in Houston, Texas. A platform was staged at the center of the stadium, where the preacher would deliver his sermon.

After the preacher delivered his message, the people in the auditorium who had not received Christ were invited to come forward and gather around the platform. Once they reached the platform, Christian counselors would come and stand behind each individual, and once they were dismissed, they walked across the field, where there were chairs set up, facing one another.

This night, Marge, who was one of the counselors, walked down and stood behind a lady whom she later found out was Pam, who was a flight attendant. While standing behind Pam, Marge noticed a man coming up to the side who had on dirty coveralls, and he had oily, dirty, stringy long hair. He was filthy looking.

Then Sam, one of the college students from Marge's class, came and stood behind him. When they were dismissed, they walked over to where the chairs were. Sam sat in front of the man dressed in dirty coveralls, and Marge and Pam sat down and faced each other.

Marge said, "Oh, Pam, tell me what your decision is."

She said, "I would like to ask Jesus to come into my heart."

Marge said, "That's wonderful."

So, Marge got the Bible out and showed her a scripture concerning salvation, and Pam then went ahead and asked Jesus to come into her life. Then after Marge prayed and thanked God, Pam headed back toward the stadium.

Then Sam, who had been ministering to the man in dirty coveralls, introduced Marge to him. "Marge, this is Skeeter. I need to tell you about Skeeter. He told me that he was saved. He asked Jesus to come into his heart back there. He knows that he is saved, but he can't be forgiven."

Marge said, "Oh, Skeeter, when you asked Jesus Christ to come into your heart, all your sins from the time you were born until now are forgiven. He cleanses you from all unrighteousness and sin."

Skeeter responded, "You don't understand, lady."

Marge said, "If you would tell me, I would like to understand."

He said, "Lady, you don't understand."

So, Marge told him about the thief on the cross who was forgiven. She told him everything that she could think of that might help him, but Skeeter kept saying, "You don't understand!"

Marge said, "Would you tell me what's wrong so I can understand?"

Skeeter said, "I can't tell you. I can't tell anybody!"

Marge said, "Oh, Skeeter, you know what? If you genuinely asked Jesus Christ to come into your heart, then He forgave you. But the problem is that you are just not aware of the forgiveness that God has already given you. Let's sit down here, you and me, and Sam will sit right here, and I want you to pray that God will open your heart and let you see that you are truly forgiven. And then I'll pray."

Skeeter, who was troubled in his mind and in his emotions, prayed slowly and sincerely, "God, I don't see how you can forgive me, but if you can…" Skeeter stopped in the middle of his prayer and looked up at Marge, and with a broken heart, he said, "Lady, He can't forgive me."

Marge said, "Would you mind telling me why?"

He said, "I'm a member of the mafia in Houston. I just shoot people and leave them there."

Marge was taken by surprise and thought to herself, *Boy, that's a biggie!* But knowing that God's forgiveness is perfect, she said, "Let's pray. God can even forgive that. Our God can forgive anything."

So Skeeter went on praying, "God, if that lady's right and you can forgive me of the horrible things I've done and have been doing so long, oh, God, let me know you really forgive me."

Then Marge thanked God and prayed, "God, I know you're bigger than any sin that any of us has or any collection of sins. Lord, you're bigger than that. God, please help Skeeter to know that he's forgiven, in Jesus's name. Amen."

Then Skeeter jumped straight up, held his hands out, and then ran toward the stadium and then made a U-turn and ran screaming, "I'm forgiven! I'm forgiven! Oh, God, I'm really forgiven!" He came back to Marge and said, "Lady, you've got to pray for me. I'm going to the mafia right now in just a minute, and I'm going to tell them that I want out." Marge knew you couldn't get out of the mafia alive. She said, "Skeeter, I know a six-foot-eight policeman who is a good friend. Please let me—"

Skeeter interrupted, "You'll get me killed."

Marge said, "Skeeter, we'll pray for you. I'll be gone for a week. I'm leaving in the morning, and I'll check on you when we get back."

Marge got Skeeter's address and asked Dole, their minister of education, to check on him while she was out of town. She was gone for about a week, and when she came home, she asked Dole about Skeeter.

Dole said, "I've got good news and bad news. The bad news, Marge, is when he told them he wanted out and that he was forgiven by God and that he never wanted to do anything like that ever again, they tied him feet first behind a tractor, facedown, and dragged him from one vacant lot to another, shredded him on the front, turned him over, and shredded him on the back, and he is in the hospital, dying. Marge, I'm glad you didn't see him. You wouldn't have recognized him. He was absolutely mutilated. I walked in that room, and I said, 'Marge Caldwell said to tell you hello and that she loves you.'"

What was the good news?

Skeeter said, "Tell that lady, I'm forgiven."

Billy Moore

Billy Moore confessed to murdering an elderly man during a robbery. Before being sentenced to death row, Billy was visited by two Christians who explained that forgiveness and hope are available through Christ. Billy said, "Nobody ever told me that Jesus loves me and died for me."

Billy went on to say, "It was a love I could feel. It was a love I wanted. It was a love I needed." Billy was baptized in a bathtub outside his cell, and God began to change him from the inside out. He took dozens of Bible courses by correspondence and began counseling other inmates and even troubled teenagers sent to him by local churches.

For sixteen years, he was a humble missionary inside the prison, "a saintly figure" in the words of the *Atlanta Journal Constitution*.

In fact, he became so thoroughly transformed that the Georgia Parole and Pardon Board ended up doing something unprecedented: they opened up the gates of death row and set him free.

Today, he's an ordained minister, a man of compassion and prayer who spends his time helping people who are hurting and forgotten.

Billy Moore said, "Plain and simple, it was Jesus Christ. He changed me in ways I could never have changed on my own. He gave me a reason to live. He helped me do the right thing. He gave me a heart for others. He saved my soul."

Serge LeClerc

Serge LeClerc was born of a fifteen-year-old country girl who ran away from home because she had been sexually abused by her grandfather and, in turn, by her father.

Then, like many damaged young girls, she fell for the first man who showed any interest in her. He immediately left upon finding out that she was pregnant.

Serge was born in a summer resort in the middle of winter, and when he was born, his mother cut the umbilical cord with her own teeth.

His mother was an illiterate French country girl, neither knowing how to read nor write. Because she couldn't speak the English language properly, she had to work very menial jobs as a dishwasher and an elevator operator, where she worked eighty hours a week. As a result of these low-paying jobs, she could only afford to move into the ghetto of Toronto's Cabbage town.

At eight years old, Serge did what many kids did in his neighborhood: he played hooky from school. Under the Juvenile Delinquents Act of that day, playing hooky from school meant that you fell into a category called the status offense. It also applied to a child from a single-parent home, a child whose parent had a problem with alcohol, a child who came from an abusive home, or a child who came from poverty.

They took Serge's mother and sat her in juvenile court and called her an unfit mother—an unfit mother for having the gall to be poor and not having a husband! This was a woman who went to church twice a week and never hit Serge in anger, and yet the verdict was that she was an unfit mother.

Serge was only able to see his mother once in the next three years. They put Serge in a training school, and the training school in that era was a humongous affair consisting of five hundred to six hundred boys. Because there was such a high number of children, the older and tougher boys would control the younger and weaker ones.

In the training school, there was wholesale brutality, beatings, rape, and solitary confinement. Serge had never been exposed to that type of brutality at the hands of an adult and, therefore, decided to run away.

He became a street child—a street child with a lot of ghetto-boy sense. He realized that if he stayed off the streets at night, he had a better chance in staying free from the people who were supposed to take care of him. He was learning that the people who were put in charge to care for him didn't care! He learned that if he was going to survive, he had to care less than everybody else.

Serge lived in abandoned houses or boxcars, cornfields, and underneath porches. He would eat out of garbage cans in the back of restaurants. He did whatever it took to survive.

Serge would eventually be rearrested because somebody would notice this tattered little boy. When he went back to training school, the brutality became worse because he was diagnosed as defiant.

Eventually, Serge escaped again but was rearrested two years later. He knew that this time, he was really going to get a dose of "care."

A staff member took a dislike to Serge. He made Serge his special project. He would have his way with Serge in his office. Two months short of his tenth birthday, Serge went to the table and broke off a prong from a pitchfork and wrapped it with a cloth at its end. When the staff member came on shift that night, sure enough, he called Serge into his office to show him how much he cared. Before he could do so, Serge stabbed him.

In a state of desperation and hopelessness, this little boy attacked a full-grown man. Serge learned that you didn't have to care at all in order to stab somebody.

Serge was sent to a foster home in the ghetto of Cabbage town, to a bungalow with twelve other children. The family was supplementing their income by taking children in. Both people who were in charge— the people who were supposed to show care for the children—were alcoholics. Serge realized that this was just another facility and that he was better off and much safer to be with people who didn't care for him. So out the bedroom window he went to be a street child.

By the time he was twelve, he carried a straight razor. Later, by the time he was sixteen years old, that straight razor turned into a gun.

When Serge was fifteen years old, he became the leader of a large street gang called the Bowery. Grown men, as old as twenty-five, would take orders from this fifteen-year-old kid. Why? Because he was good at what he did and because he didn't care. He was becoming hard. Getting sliced open or a broken nose in a street fight was a common occurrence.

Serge began a twenty-year odyssey of drug use, seven years of it as a heroin addict. He was a mainline user, not only living in hell but pumping hell into himself.

Serge in Prison

Serge, wired out of his mind on drugs and thinking he was Jesse James, was eventually arrested for violating the law. The police put a tag on him when they sent him through the system, which said, "This kid doesn't care."

Since he didn't care, they sent him to maximum security at the tender age of about eighteen or nineteen years old. Upon entering maximum security, this well-muscled weightlifter adult decided that Serge couldn't be as bad as they said. So, he decided that he was going to make Serge his sexual play toy.

Serge said to the man, "Go get your knife because that's not going to happen. One of us is going to die."

Because Serge didn't care, he stabbed that man seven times and took his lung out for him. Then when they were dragging him to solitary confinement, he made the mistake of lashing out and breaking a guard's jaw.

Solitary Confinement

Serge spent the next twenty-seven months in solitary confinement in a six-by-nine cement cell. He wasn't allowed out for showers or fresh air. He wasn't allowed to talk to anyone or to even read.

They singled him out for special treatment. They would rip his clothes off and hog-tie him. Then they would connect chains to the shackles on his feet and pull them onto the handcuffs on his back until his legs were bent up and his heels were touching his buttocks. He couldn't move on his side because he would rip his shoulders out. At one time, they left him there like that for ten days, and he had to eat his bologna sandwiches out of a paper plate face-first like a dog.

Serge learned what it was to hate. He became one of the most feared and vicious men in the prison system as he killed, beat, and maimed his way through existence year after year. When he was eventually released from prison, he carried his fierce lifestyle out into the streets. He became very good at being a criminal. He became an organized-crime figure.

Serge did business with mafia godfathers who wined and dined him. He controlled Québec and Ontario for designer drugs, methamphetamine, and acid; and he controlled 50 percent of the flow of hashish. You didn't do business with Serge LeClerc unless you had a million dollars. Anything less would be chump change. It wasn't worth it—to take too great a chance for too little profit. He had no compulsion whatsoever of spilling ten or fifteen million dollars' worth of drugs to pollute the veins and minds of children. He didn't care! He lived off hate. He was as hard as hard could be, and he was as dysfunctional as any human being could ever be.

Then once again, Serge was arrested and sent back to the penitentiary. When Serge walked into this maximum security in Québec, a young twenty-five-year-old weightlifter decided that he was going to rise a little bit in the power structure and deal with this man called Serge LeClerc. But he found himself on the working end of a three-foot table leg.

Once again, Serge found himself in solitary confinement. It was nothing new because he had already spent about six years of his life there. It was a home away from home in prison. When he got stressed out, he would go into this hole for two to three months just to rest.

Serge LeClerc's Conversion

The order was given. "No one is to go near Serge LeClerc's cell!" Serge was just as prone to punch a guard in the mouth as he was an inmate.

Then, as Serge sat in his cell, he began noticing an event. He would stare out his door and would watch a strange little man come in twice a week. He would go around to the other cells and would spend five or ten minutes talking to each inmate and would hand out magazines.

Serge watched this man as day turned into week and week turned into month and month started going on to a year. He watched this man come in every week. He later found out that the man was a Christian.

Serge thought, *this man is kooky. How would anybody subject themselves to this type of humiliation? To do what? To talk to one of the scum in this hole. This man's weird!*

Finally, Serge called him over to his cell, and this little man almost went into shock. There was a strict order not to come near his cell. When Serge was escorted to the yard, they would put shackles on him; and before he was allowed to walk into the yard, he had to stick his arms through a door to get a pair of handcuffs put on him.

So, this Christian came over to his cell and was about to go into a seizure. He began talking a mile a minute. He saw his opening. He began talking to Serge about the popular Christian speaker Billy Graham and started talking to him about God.

Serge said, "Whoa! I don't want to hear about Billy Graham. All he's doing is pushing another product. I don't want to hear about God. There is no God! Don't tell me about God!"

Serge continued, "I just want to tell you I kind of respect you. I think, in your own weird way, you care. I just wanted to tell you that. Next month, I'm being shipped out, and before I left, I just wanted to tell you that even though I think you're weird, you're a good guy."

Then just as the Christian was leaving, he took a step away from the door and then had a second thought and reached back and handed Serge some magazines.

Without thinking, Serge grabbed the magazines. "Whoa, Christian magazines. I can't have this!" He threw them into the corner of his cell.

Later, Serge went down to the steam wagon and got his supper tray and came back. In solitary confinement, there are no tables, and you're not allowed anything but a plastic spoon, so sometimes eating becomes difficult. This night, he got bored with his meal. He began wandering around his cell, and suddenly, when he came out of his daze, his eyes were fixed on the top magazine cover.

When he looked, he noticed a picture on the front of it. The picture was of a fellow by the name of Roy Hill, a man whom Serge grew up with. He was a person who did at least fifteen years in the prison system for just beating up guards and police officers. He was one of the toughest men Serge knew with his fists.

Serge thought, *what is he doing on the cover of a Christian magazine? This guy must have blown it. He must have gone off the deep end.*

Serge's curiosity was aroused, so he read the article about Roy Hill. Roy told about his life story. His life story was very similar to the life story of most people in prison. You just change some of the components. He talked about his mother being a prostitute and how she was an alcoholic. He told about how he became a street child and, eventually, an alcoholic. He talked about how he was consumed by hate and how people never cared.

As Serge was reading the article, he realized that it was all the same thing. It was the same story until he got to his last statement: "It's all changed. For the first time in my life, I know peace of mind, and I know freedom since I came to know God." Serge laughed to himself and said, "Aah, just burned out." But that statement would come back and haunt Serge LeClerc; and eventually, it would come back and save him.

In the cell beside Serge was a nineteen-year-old boy who was doing fourteen years for robbing three pizza establishments with an unloaded shotgun. Since he was Serge's next-door neighbor, he would talk to Serge a lot. He talked about his life story, about being abandoned at two years old, being a street child, a juvenile delinquent, about reform school, and about now standing in a federal prison—one of the toughest maximums—because he stabbed somebody who wanted to rape him.

He would tell Serge, "Nobody cared!"

Serge would answer him, "Kid, you're right. Nobody cares. No one. Not even me. I don't care. You better learn not to care if you want to survive. You care less than anyone else. You care less until you don't even care about life anymore. Because that's the only way you're going to make it!"

Three weeks later, Serge listened to that boy hang himself. The sound of him hanging and choking his life out was a sound Serge could never forget. He knew it was so final.

As they took his body past Serge's cell on a stretcher, he suddenly realized that he had been screaming on the inside, *Kid, you shouldn't have done it! Because if nobody else cared, I care!*

It blew Serge's mind. All his life, he had lived off hate and not caring. The thought of caring about whether another human being hanged himself was so alien to him that it really drove him around the bend.

Serge refused to come out of his cell. He refused to eat or go to work. His friends became worried about him. Usually, in his past pattern of behavior, if he went into hibernation, he was psyching himself up to go to war.

A friend of Serge's, who was doing twenty-four years and was also an organized-crime figure and martial arts expert, stopped by the front of Serge's cell with concern and said, "I'm worried about you, Serge."

Serge said, "You know, I'm kind of worried about myself." He said, "Are you psyching yourself up to go to war?"

Serge answered, "No, I'm just bummed out. I don't know what's happening to me."

All during this time, Serge kept hearing the echo, "For the first time in my life, I know peace of mind and freedom since I've come to know God." It kept echoing and wouldn't go away.

Then a friend of Serge's said, "Why don't you come to the chapel with me."

Serge answered, "Chapel! What! Are you nuts? You're not a Christian."

He said, "No, I'm not. But it's one of the few places in this insane asylum where I don't have to worry about getting stabbed in the back."

Serge asked, "What do you do there?"

He answered, "Well, we have coffee and doughnuts."

Serge responded, "Well, that's nothing to run out on a rainy day for.

What else do you do there?"

"Well, we sing songs."

"You sing like a frog. Do you mean I have to go and hear you sing like a frog? It's not too appetizing right now. What else?"

He said, "You know, Serge, it's a strange thing. I've been watching these people come in here for the last number of months through snowstorms to talk to the guys. You know, I think they really care."

The magic words. Serge had to see this strange animal who truly cared. Almost two years later, on a cold cement prison floor, Serge asked Jesus to come into his life.

Serge was thirty-five years old on Christmas Day morning in 1985, and everything turned around. A twenty-year-old drug dependency immediately stopped with that decision.

Later, Serge LeClerc received a full pardon and was giving his life in helping others. He founded and became the director of a chapel of prison fellowship in Canada, and his testimony is helping people around the world.

Duane and Iris Blue

As a rebellious young thirteen-year-old, Iris would get arrested for various crimes and would be released into the custody of her parents. When she got a little older, she began working at topless nightclubs. She also began doing drugs and stealing and was eventually arrested for armed robbery. This time, they didn't release her into the custody of her parents. Because of the seriousness of the crime, they kept her in jail until she could be tried as an adult.

She stayed in jail for nine months and went through horrible withdrawal symptoms. After nine months in jail, she was sentenced to eight years in prison. She was told that she could get out soon on good behavior, but she never was good. She was released after a total of seven years.

Her dad picked her up in prison, while her mother was at home, fixing her a smorgasbord of food. But she wanted a hamburger on the way home. She hadn't ridden in a car for seven years, so when she got in the car with the hamburger's grease running down her elbow, she got sick.

They pulled over to the side of the road, and her dad grabbed his handkerchief and wrapped some ice with it and put it on her head. Her dad began telling her that she was the spirit of Christmas and his star on the tree and that she was his Easter Bunny. Regardless of the bad things she had done in her life, her father knew that she was Daddy's little girl.

Years earlier, when she had gotten into a knife fight, she was given a psychological test and personality evaluation and was diagnosed as an incorrigible and a degenerate. This meant that she was incapable of being corrected or amended; this person was worse than a pervert. But her father wouldn't give up on her.

Within hours of her prison release, Iris was back on drugs. When she came home, even though she was high, her mother marched her to her bedroom, and on her bed was piled seven years' worth of Christmas presents, Valentine's Day presents, Easter baskets, and birthday presents.

Iris came from a good home, from a mother and father who loved her with no strings attached. Although they loved her unconditionally, Iris was stubborn in her ways. Once again, Iris began working in bars and eventually ran three nightclubs.

Iris's mother prayed fervently for her. In fact, she had her whole church praying. She prayed, "God, whatever it takes, save my baby. I don't want to go to heaven without her."

Two weeks later, a Christian man heard a message in church that we, as Christians, are to be a lighthouse to the people of this world who are without God. Just as a farmer is looking, ready, and expecting to bring a harvest in—we, as Christians, should be looking to bring a harvest of lost souls to God.

So, this Christian man chose Iris. Somebody said to him, "Leave Iris alone. She's a troublemaker!" He responded, "If Jesus can save me, He can save her."

So, he began witnessing to Iris. He would give her pamphlets with verses of scripture on them. He would tell her how valuable she was. He would tell her, "You're so valuable. If you were the only person in the world, Jesus would have died for you. God loves you, Iris."

He would call the bar late at night. Iris would be buzzing on drugs and would have to head to the bathroom because of the loudness of the bar so she could hear what he had to say. He would say, "I just called to tell you you're not going to believe what I just read, 'Jesus loves you.'" And then she would hang up on him.

While he witnessed to her from Sunday through Thursday, Iris and her girlfriends at the bar had a plan of their own. They tried luring him into sexual sin. Finally, he called Iris and said, "Iris, would you meet me outside? I won't ever witness to you again. I just want to say bye."

She went out and sat in his car. He said, "Iris, I can't see you anymore because I made a commitment a long time ago that I wasn't going to mess with any tramps. I wasn't going to be around any."

When he called Iris a tramp, she wanted to cut his throat. All week, he had been telling her that she was valuable and precious, and in one word, he called her garbage.

In the next breath, he said, "You think I'm not a man because of what you girls are trying to get me to do. I won't go for it. I know it would feel good for a few moments, but I am more concerned about your eternity than a moment of pleasure for me."

Iris thought, *I have met men who would ruin anybody's life for a few moments of pleasure, and yet this man is concerned about my eternity?*

The Christian man began weeping and said, "Iris, Jesus can make you a lady."

When he said the word *lady*, it was like something busted open, and she said, "I want it!" She wanted it so bad, she couldn't stand it.

He then explained to her that receiving Jesus is like a marriage ceremony. It's like saying "I do." He said, "The King of kings wants all of you. Are you ready?"

Iris said, "I'm ready!"

He said, "If you mean business, let's pray outside on this street corner." So, they knelt on the street corner. He didn't trust her yet, so when he prayed, he kept one eye open. He said, "Jesus, do you want her? Jesus said yes." (Iris didn't hear anything, but that's what he told her.) He said, "Iris, do you want Jesus?"

She said, "Yeah, I do."

He said, "Jesus, you know what it takes to get this gal. She isn't worth anything. You really want her? Oh, He really wants you, Iris.

Whatever it takes, He wants you. Do you want Him?"

Iris said, "I do."

He said, "Well, repeat these words after me: I, Iris, give myself to you." And he led her in a sinner's prayer. She knelt on that street corner as a tramp but then stood as a lady—clean, pure, and forgiven.

Iris's Future Husband, Duane Blue

Duane Blue was born in Denver, Colorado, and lived there for two years. After his father left his mother, he moved with her to Kalamazoo, Michigan, where he grew up. This is where he rode motorcycles, quit school, and got into drugs.

Blue was a liar and a thief who abused his mother. He never hit her; he would abuse her with his words. He would call her filthy names, knowing that she would cry and go into the bathroom, and then he could do whatever he wanted.

Later, when he lived away from home, he knew that at 3:00 p.m., she would be sorting mail at the post office and wouldn't come home till 11:00 p.m. at night. So, at times, he would break into her home and steal from her.

When Blue was twenty-one years old, he kicked in her door one afternoon, made himself a sandwich, turned on the stereo, and called his buddies and said, "Light 'em up, boys. We're going to party till 11:00 p.m. We can do anything we want. She's at work."

Before his friends got to the house that day, Blue walked into the bathroom and found his mother's body on the floor. She took over two hundred pills to kill herself. She committed suicide because of her son.

Blue never went to her funeral. The day she was buried, Blue got so drunk he just wanted that day to go away. Without ever visiting his mother's grave, he moved to Houston, Texas.

Blue had a beard that was down about the middle of his waist, and his hair was past his waist. He lived in a 1952 International School bus with two large German shepherd dogs that went everywhere he went. They went to work with him, and they went to the bars with him.

He drove a three-wheeled motorcycle with a Volkswagen van engine in the back and a Triumph motorcycle in the front. It had three seats altogether—a big saddle seat up front and two Ford van seats over the wheels in the back. When he would say "Load up," his dogs would get into those backseats. When he went to work, he would say "Stay," and his dogs would remain there until he got back.

Blue Meets Iris

Earnest, a coworker who worked with Blue, walked up to him two weeks before Christmas and said, "Blue, I'd like you to come home with me for the Christmas holidays. You need to meet my sister. She used to be a liar and a thief like you."

After Blue accepted his invitation, Earnest called his sister, Iris, in Atlanta, Georgia, and said, "Sister, don't bring home any weirdos with you this year. I already have one. This boy I'm bringing home lives in a bus with a bunch of dogs. It's hard to tell who's the hairiest between him and the dogs. He has a filthy mouth, and he doesn't even know how to read. I just wanted you to know I'm bringing him. Don't buy him any books or anything. We don't want to embarrass him."

So, Blue brought his dogs with him to Atlanta, Georgia. He figured that if they didn't like him, it didn't matter. His plan was to eat their food, sleep in a nice bed for a couple of nights. He was going to get stoned, sit in their living room, and watch the Christmas tree blink. He was going to take everything he could get from them, and when he was through, he would leave.

When they started passing out gifts from under the tree, they handed Blue a gift. He didn't expect a gift from anybody. When he opened the present, it was the Bible on cassette tapes and a cassette player to go with it.

All Blue wanted to know was who gave him those so he could shove it down their throat. He asked Earnest, "Who gave me these?" He smiled and said, "My sister got those for you."

Blue waited for his opportunity. He was going to teach Iris a lesson she would never forget. He already knew about Iris's past. He learned from working with her brother, Earnest, that she had been a prostitute, a heroin addict, had abortions, and served time in prison.

Blue was good at mental abuse. He had a lot of practice on his mother. He knew how to hurt people. He started as a thirteen-year-old boy in his mother's home until the time he was twenty-one and did all the damage his mother could stand.

He thought, *I'll have her weeping before it's over. She'll run to her bedroom, and then I'll get on my three-wheeler with my dogs and get out of here. She needs a good lesson!*

Finally, his opportunity arrived. He saw that Iris was alone in the living room, sitting on the couch. So he went over and sat beside her and then proceeded to tell her every filthy thing he knew about her.

But Blue was taken by surprise when she said with cheerful enthusiasm, "That's true. I'm going to a church this Sunday to share that story. Why don't you come with me?"

Then Blue came up with another plan. *I'll go and teach this woman a lesson she will never forget. This is going to be great.*

Blue normally never cut or trimmed his beard. It stuck out all over the place at different lengths. He wore three rubber bands in his hair so it wouldn't get in a knot. But for church, he pulled all three of them out and let it hang everywhere. He put on his favorite T-shirt with a hole so big you could see his stomach right through it. He took a brush and ran it through his beard so that it was puffed up as big as he could get it to be. He thought about putting a plastic spider in it. He figured that when she saw him, she was going to have a heart attack and never take him to church.

But Blue was surprised once again when she pulled in and picked him up at his bus and acted like nothing was wrong. She just began talking to him and making conversation, asking what he had done that week, asking him how he trained his dogs to stay on the motorcycle. She asked him all kinds of questions, and before he knew it, he was in a church parking lot.

They went in through the two doors in the back of the church. About the second row from the back, this tiny little old lady stepped right out into the aisle in front of Blue, put her hand out, and looked up at him, grinning, and said, "We're glad to see you today!"

Blue took a seat, and during the church service, he listened to Iris share her testimony. He was amazed at how open and honest she was about the horrible life she lived before she became a Christian.

When she was finished, a preacher got up and said, "Maybe you're here today and you're a sinner."

Blue knew he was a sinner. He was a liar, a thief, and a bully. He couldn't read, but he figured that book they were holding probably said that some have lied, stolen, abused their family, done drugs, and fallen short of the glory of God. He eventually came to find out that it said, "All have sinned." He thought he was a sinner because he was wicked. He didn't know he was a sinner simply because he was born.

Iris gave Blue her card and said, "If you ever want to talk to me, you can call me at any time. I don't care if it's late at night."

When Blue got back to his bus, he told his dogs, "Load up." He got on his motorcycle and went cruising through the park where everybody pointed at him, and he could be the center of attention. Blue said, "Forget that lady. She's crazy."

Blue was a man who went to the bar every single night. Everybody in the bar knew him. Nobody would even park in his section where his two dogs would be sitting. That was his parking spot.

It had been two weeks since Blue went to church with Iris. The bar closed on this night, but he still wasn't quite drunk enough to go to sleep. He wasn't drunk enough to forget his past. There was no present to look at, and there never was going to be a future. He hated seeing his mother's body in his mind repeatedly.

So, he decided to call Iris, and they talked for a long time. Then he finally got tired, went to his bus, went to sleep, and then got up and went to work. A couple of weeks later, he called her again. Then a couple of weeks later, he called her two times—and a week after that, every single night of the week.

Then one night, Iris said to him, "Blue, what would you do if you were standing in a church at an altar getting married?" (Blue knew he would never be married. He thought that women were something you use. You don't keep them.)

She said, "What if you met a real lady who wanted to be your wife? Pretend you're standing in a church and the preacher said to you, 'Blue, do you take this woman to be your wife?'"

Blue held the phone. He didn't say anything.

She said, "You would be nervous, but you would say, 'I do.' But what if the lady you are marrying said, 'I got this other boyfriend named Tom. I'm going to marry Blue, but every Friday night, when I tuck Blue into bed,

I'm going to slip over to Tom's house and sleep with him. You know, it's just a physical thing with me and Tom.'"

Blue started yelling at her over the phone, "You're crazy, lady! You think I would marry some girl who would sleep with some other guy and tell me this at the altar! That's stupid, lady!"

Iris said, "You wouldn't accept her commitment?"

Blue answered, "That's not a commitment. That is trash!"

She said, "What do you think God will do with your commitment?"

For the first time in his life, he realized it's not just a matter of believing in Jesus. It's a commitment of your life.

Finally, his heart broke. With all sincerity, this big hairy man on the parking lot pay phone said to Iris, "Lady, I don't know how to pray! I don't know how to talk to God. I don't even know how to read. I don't know anything. For thirty-three years, lady, I've been living for me. If God's real, I want to live for Him."

The light was turned on for Duane Blue. He realized at that moment that you can lie to your mother. You can lie and steal from your biker buddies. You can lie to yourself. But you can never lie to Jesus. Jesus knew that Blue was a liar, a thief, and the murderer of his own mother. But while Duane Blue was yet in his sins, Jesus died for him. While hanging on the cross, Jesus was saying, "Duane Blue, I love you, and I'm dying for you!"

Duane Blue Living for God

Blue made a commitment to Jesus Christ in the parking lot of that bar. He joined the local church the very next Sunday.

He met his first pastor on a Thursday when he drove into the parking lot of the church. He told the pastor, "I just got saved, sir. I don't know anything about church, and I don't know anything about preachers. I always figured you were the laziest men on earth because you only work one day a week. Since today is Thursday and you're not doing anything anyway—wherever you go, sir, I'm going."

The pastor's eyes bugged out of his head. Blue went with the pastor into the hospital as he ministered to the sick. He had lunch with the pastor as he sat with his other preacher friends.

That first Sunday morning, Blue sat on the front row and cried through the whole service. He cried when the pastor explained to him that the big hairy boy has died and there was now a little boy who is alive and could grow in Jesus and become something.

Blue attended every church service and got involved in every activity they had going. He wanted to get involved in anything Jesus was doing.

Later, Duane and Iris got married. They have given their lives to the work of the Lord. They are spending their lives sharing their testimonies and are helping people come to the saving knowledge of the Lord Jesus Christ. If God can save the Blues, He can save anybody.

About the Author

RICKY TUTOR BEGAN his journey with the Lord in September of 1980. Not too long after his conversion, his desire to find out what it's all about began to grow. In over forty years of study, this desire has not left him to this very day.

Eventually, he realized that the desire he had was a God-given desire. His desire, plus his ability to write books, revealed his calling—sharing with others what it's all about. His first book, *What It's All About*, was published in 2007. This book advanced into a larger book called *Doing the Will of the Father*, which was published in 2010. *The God Journey* book is the perfected and more advanced version of both these books.

Ricky Tutor was born in Sardis, Mississippi, but has lived most of his life in the state of Illinois. He and his wife, Donna, live in Joliet, Illinois. They are members of the Word of Life Church, Crest Hill, Illinois.